COMUS AND SOME SHORTER POEMS
OF MILTON

COMUS AND SOME SHORTER POEMS
OF MILTON
Edited by E. M. W. TILLYARD, Litt.D.
Master of Jesus College, Cambridge,

and

PHYLLIS B. TILLYARD, M.A.
Girton College, Cambridge

CHAUCER: THE PROLOGUE TO THE
CANTERBURY TALES
Edited by R. T. DAVIES, M.A., Lecturer in English,
Liverpool University

CHAUCER: THE KNIGHT'S TALE
Edited by J. A. W. BENNETT, D. Phil.,
Fellow of Magdalen College, Oxford

APOLLO AND DAPHNE
by Tiepolo

Comus
and Some Shorter Poems
of Milton

EDITED WITH AN INTRODUCTION BY

E. M. W. TILLYARD LITT.D.
Master of Jesus College, Cambridge

AND WITH NOTES BY

PHYLLIS B. TILLYARD M.A.
Girton College, Cambridge

GEORGE G. HARRAP *&* CO. LTD
LONDON TORONTO WELLINGTON SYDNEY

First published 1952
by GEORGE G. HARRAP & CO. LTD
182 High Holborn, London, W.C.1
Reprinted 1953

*Composed in Garamond type and printed by
Western Printing Services Ltd, Bristol*

Made in Great Britain

PREFACE

EVERY annotator of Milton except the first must owe something to his predecessors. For this edition these works have been especially helpful: H. J. Todd's edition of Milton's poems "with notes of various authors," sometimes known as Todd's variorum edition; Aldis Wright's facsimile of the Milton manuscript in Trinity College, Cambridge; R. C. Browne's edition of the poems; A. W. Verity's edition of the poems; Merritt Y. Hughes' edition of the poems; B. A. Wright's *Shorter Poems of John Milton*; J. S. Smart's edition of the sonnets. It is regretted that W. J. Halliday's edition of Milton's minor poems came to our notice too late to be consulted.

Thanks are due to the National Gallery of Art, Washington, D.C., for kind permission to reproduce Tiepolo's picture of Apollo pursuing Daphne.

E.M.W.T.
P.B.T.

CONTENTS

INTRODUCTION

INTRODUCTION

I. General

THIS edition of Milton's shorter poems is meant for school use, and as such it is open to the challenge: "Why should Milton's shorter poems be studied in schools at all?" The first and obvious answer is: because they are a set book for a Certificate Examination. And for many people who have resigned themselves to the authority of examining bodies that may be a complete and sufficient answer. But it will not satisfy all. The grounds of school education have been questioned and altered in the last fifty years in a quite new way. At the beginning of the century the assumption that mathematics (including Euclid), Latin, and Greek, and perhaps English grammar, were the grounds was paramount, controlling teacher and pupil alike. And a very comforting assumption it was, making it impossible for a schoolboy, however much he disliked a particular lesson, to think that he ought to be learning something else. It could not be a waste of time, for instance, to learn by heart a rhymed list of Latin nouns of the common gender. But in the last fifty years all this has changed. New subjects have arrived, and fight with old subjects for their quota of periods in the week. Old subjects are taught in a new way. And, in general, experiment has taken the place of a rigid certainty. And so it is likely that not every one to-day can willingly accept Milton's shorter poems as a school subject for no further reasons than that they are a set book. What

are the further reasons? For if I did not think they existed
I would not be taking a hand in this edition at all.

One reason (and it is a very strong one) is that Milton's
shorter poems have been for many years, and still are, part
of a stock of knowledge common to educated people. The
question here of whether or not you like these poems does
not come in. That a man dislikes detective fiction is no
excuse for his not knowing who Sherlock Holmes and Dr
Watson are. A man with no ear for music ought to know
when Bach and Mozart and Brahms lived. However un-
observant by nature, an educated man ought to be made to
see the difference between an Early English and a Perpendi-
cular Gothic arch. All these matters belong to that store of
common knowledge which, quite apart from taste or in-
clination, binds people together in society, giving them a
common means of communication. A London University
professor, lecturing on Milton, found among the signatures
of students attending the two following: "Comus B.
Blode" and "Lycidas B. Blode." You may think that if
the signatories felt like that about Milton's shorter poems
they had better have studied something else. But not
necessarily. They had common ground for argument with
those who felt otherwise about these poems, and they were
better off than if they had studied something unknown to
all the rest.

Milton's shorter poems are not only *classics*, in the sense
that some knowledge of them is expected in an educated
person; they contain references to matters of fact or belief
that should be familiar to him. Whether or not a person
has the slightest use for poetry as such he ought to know
the traditional conception of the music of the spheres, the
Ptolemaic and the Copernican conceptions of the universe,
the reason why St Peter carried keys, the legend of Circe
turning the followers of Odysseus into animals. All these

commonplaces crop up in Milton's shorter poems, and, even if you think you have little use for poetry as such, you will not be wasting your time if you make these poems the occasion of your general education.

But the number of people who really have no use for poetry need be very small indeed, even if the number of those who have never given it a real chance is very great. In my preparatory school we used, in the week before we broke up, to chant a set of verses beginning with the line, "This time next week where shall I be?" These were a kind of ballad material, common to most such schools, and I cannot think that they are not still chanted to-day, though the details may have changed. Naturally, the lines enumerated the things the boys were to escape from:

> No more Latin, no more Greek,
> No more canes to make me squeak;
> No more dirty bread and butter;
> No more water from the gutter;
> No more marmalade with flies;
> No more flabby apple-pies.

Apart from a new boy or two who were shocked at the rebelliousness of some of the sentiments I cannot think of anyone who had the least difficulty with this poem. No one objected to it as poetry; and poetry, even if not of a high order, it certainly is. And it is poetry because it conveys a considerable proportion of its feeling through the regular arrangement and the sound of the words. The poem is about the feelings of rebelliousness that all people have when they are under discipline, and which grow more acute as the discipline is prolonged. The acuteness of the feeling comes out partly in the exaggerated statement and partly in the pounding beat of the verse and the repetitions. The step from these verses to Milton's *L'Allegro*, which also has four beats to the line, should not be too difficult to make: in this couplet,

> Oft listening how the hounds and horn
> Cheerly rouse the slumbering Morn,

there is a powerful beat on "cheerly," expressing joyful excitement; and, in this quatrain,

> And the milkmaid singeth blithe,
> And the mower whets his scythe,
> And every shepherd tells his tale
> Under the hawthorn in the dale,

there is the same sort of lively emphasis in the repeated "and's" as in the "no more's" of the prep. school verses. *L'Allegro* may be better poetry, but the principle to which both pieces of verse go back is the same. And, if some one is at home with the simpler piece, he is well on his way to enjoying the more complicated.

But, even if some poetry is in reach of most people, should it be taught, as poetry, in schools? If there were other places where it could be taught effectively I might answer no. If most pupils grew up in families where poetry was much quoted and read, coming to learn the feel of it as they learnt to speak, then schools had better keep off the job. But, as things are, for most pupils school is the only medium. If they are not confronted with poetry at school they will go through life without the chance of getting to know one of the best things life has to offer.

Granted that poetry, as poetry, should be taught in schools, it will be found that Milton's shorter poems are eminently suited to the purpose. If you want to make a beginning with poetry you had better take something as poetical as possible, something as remote as possible from the prose of every day. There are poems, like some of Dryden's satirical or didactic pieces, that at first sight look much like versified prose. Actually they need not be, but a beginner is apt to think they are, and to feel sold if he is made to read them. They are not good for school use.

Something very varied in metre, a relatively high proportion of whose meaning is conveyed by the sound, something varied and picturesque in language, something romantic in subject, is the kind to begin on. Milton's shorter poems fulfil all these needs.

For metrical contrast what could be more striking than that between *L'Allegro* and the *Nativity Ode*: the first written in lines each containing no more and no less than four main stresses, lines moving quickly and pressing on through the poem's course to its end; the second written in a stanza containing lines of three, four, five, and six stresses, a stanza that alters its speed and does anything rather than press on evenly to its end? It is difficult to talk sensibly and clearly about sound in poetry, and I will take as obvious an instance as I can of Milton using sound to convey a high proportion of his meaning. Milton in *L'Allegro* wants to convey the swaggering gait of a cock, and his own amusement or delight in watching it, and he recounts how the cock "Stoutly struts his dames before." It is through the two emphatic beats, and the taut and crowded consonants of "stoutly struts," that the poet gives the sense of the cock's taut leg muscles and the jerky movements of raising and lowering the leg. Of course, you need the literal meaning too; but it is the sound that charges it with feeling.

Then for the language, Milton can be plain spoken when he wishes as in

> And young and old come forth to play
> On a sunshine holiday;

but his poetry is full of expressions which we (and to a lesser degree his own contemporaries) would not use in cold prose, for instance

> the drowsy frighted steeds
> That draw the litter of close-curtain'd sleep,

or the "unexpressive nuptial song." These are phrases
that suggest colour or a great occasion, and are as far as
may be from the cool element of prose; and they fit the
heightened expectation that we get from the stir of the
blood that a powerful metre should cause in us.

In his references Milton ranges romantically from earth
to heaven, and over the earth. The Attendant Spirit in
Comus comes from the "starry threshold of Jove's court";
the body of Lycidas may have been washed by the sea
"beyond the stormy Hebrides" or to the remotest Cornish
coast, where the great Archangel Michael looks out from
the mount that bears his name towards the coast of Spain;
in *Arcades* a spirit haunts the wood and listens, as no mere
human can, to the heavenly music of the spheres. All these
references are remote from prose except the romantic prose
of the fairy-tale or the adventure story. And they co-
operate with the metrical suasion and with the heightened
language to place the reader in a realm which is beyond all
doubt poetical; and in so doing they should satisfy him,
just as a fen-dweller who had never seen a mountain would,
as a first experience, prefer the Alps or the Highlands to
the South Downs.

If Milton's shorter poems are better for school study
than the poetry that is nearest prose so are they better than
the opposite extreme, the poetry that relies least on prose
content, namely the most purely lyrical. It may not be
difficult to have feelings about some of the medieval carols
or Shakespeare's or Herrick's lyrics, but in the early stages
of literary education there is very little to *say* about them.
Milton's shorter poems are both highly poetical and full of
matter that needs explanation: they must be studied as well
as enjoyed. If you go fast with them you lose much of the
sense, and with it much of the enjoyment. Take this
speech of the evil magician, Comus, to the Lady as she is

discovered sitting in the enchanted chair. She makes as if
to rise, and Comus says:

> Nay, Lady, sit; if I but wave this wand,
> Your nerves are all chained up in alablaster
> And you a statue, or as Daphne was
> Root-bound, that fled Apollo.

The gist of the lines is plain: Comus has the Lady in his
power, and she cannot escape from the chair without his
permission. But how crowded with meaning the lines are!
They begin dramatically: you can see Comus's gesture as he
says the first three words, where 'sit' means 'remain
seated,' or 'it is no use trying to get up.' Comus, as a
character, is not only an imagined figure of classical
mythology but a magician with a wand in the manner of
native fairy-tales. In the second line Milton would not have
affected the gist of the passage if he had said 'limbs' instead
of 'nerves'; and he would have said something much more
easy and obvious if he had. Chains on limbs is a familiar,
even *the* familiar, idea. But, for the very reason that he feels
more keenly than the ordinary person, Milton is moved to
say something that startles, and yet is perfectly apt. The
idea of nerves being chained is startling, yet it is the nerves
that are the agents of vitality: hence it is they and not some
other part of the body that should be imprisoned. Statues
are usually in marble or bronze, and Milton could have said
'lifeless bronze' or what not. But he chooses a rarer and
more specialized word in 'alablaster' (or as we say,
alabaster) and, like 'nerves,' it is both surprising and apt.
It is surprising compared with 'marble' or 'bronze'
because of its rarity and particularity, but to see its aptitude
you must know what alabaster is like. Alabaster is a peculiarly delicate kind of stone, slightly transparent, beautifully
soft-looking when polished, and often pinkish in colour.
Milton used the word because he wants us to think of the

texture of the Lady's skin, of her youth and freshness. He is hinting what Shakespeare put more directly when he made Othello call the sleeping Desdemona "smooth as monumental alablaster." Finally, why must Milton bring in the legend of Apollo and Daphne? There was nothing strange in this, for the legend was well known to most hearers or readers in Milton's day through the verse of Ovid, as I point out below in Section VII of this introduction. Comus uses the legend to bring home to the Lady that she is quite in his power: he can deprive her of all movement as if she were turned into wood, and, as it were, root her feet inextricably in the ground. And he also insinuates that, as Daphne came to a sad end for her coyness, so too may the Lady, thus making a prelude to his coming attack on her virtue.

So long an explanation of only three and a half lines of verse may have a discouraging air; and if *Comus* had to be studied in that sort of detail the set books could not be done in the time. But my point is that Milton's shorter poems are packed close, that there is a lot to be found out about them, that they reward study even if thorough study is out of the question. They are indeed among those rare poems which can be enjoyed in readings of different degrees of thoroughness, like Coleridge's *Ancient Mariner*, Keats's *Odes*, and Yeats's *Byzantium*: poems which give a quick return, yet which are not exhausted however much read and pondered on. A man may read them when he is quite young, and need not tire of them his whole life through.

To study such poetry at school has its penalty. In mathematics the pupil begins with easy things, which he is expected to master completely before he goes up to the more difficult; and so on throughout. But you cannot work that way with poetry, where the easy and the difficult are mixed up, and where the best schoolmaster that ever was has not got the complete answer. So you must not expect the same sort of discipline as from precise subjects like mathematics. Both kinds have their merits; and, if mathematics is more precise, poetry is more like life itself.

But, though you have to admit that in all Milton's shorter poems the simple and the profound are mixed, it is only common sense to begin with the most easily understandable. Of the poems included in this edition it is *L'Allegro* and *Il Penseroso* with which the beginnner in Milton will have least difficulty; and the teacher would do well to make his class study these before the *Navitity Ode*, even if this goes against the time sequence of composition. Anyhow, I will comment on these two poems first as being the best introduction to the bulk of the shorter poems.

II. "L'Allegro" and "Il Penseroso"

L'Allegro and *Il Penseroso* mean the cheerful and the thoughtful man respectively ('allegro' is the same word as the common musical term for 'brisk' or 'fast'); and in one sense the two poems describe the business and the pleasures of the cheerful and the thoughtful man. But there is another theme that runs through the poems—the contrasted themes of day and night; day corresponding to *L'Allegro*, and night to *Il Penseroso*. And this second theme helps us to understand why Milton should have written a poem in two parts.

But before I can explain this I must say something about when the twin poems were written. Milton entered Christ's College, Cambridge, in 1625 at the age of sixteen, and left on taking his M.A. degree in 1632. After that he went to live with his parents at Horton, in Buckinghamshire, where he continued the studies he thought necessary for his

B

education as a poet. There are a good many references to the country in *L'Allegro* and *Il Penseroso*, and for a century and a half it had become the habit to connect them with Milton's residence at Horton. There is no other evidence for this connexion, and it amounts to nothing, for we know that Milton had spent college vacations in the country, while no city in his own day, not even London of which he was a native, was beyond easy walking distance of the open fields. On the other hand there are close likenesses between *L'Allegro* and one of the Latin exercises written by Milton to fulfil the requirements of his degrees. In Milton's day these requirements were very different from what they are now. There were no printed sets of questions which the candidate had to answer in writing within a given time. Instead, he had to support or attack a given thesis in a Latin speech of his own composing before an audience of mixed dons and undergraduates. This he had to do several times during his course, and to the satisfaction of the judges in point of both matter and style. Some of the subjects set were on general topics, like the contention that silence is better than speech, others concerned technical philosophical questions. The candidate had to be prepared to talk on either side, as called on. Very few of the exercises, or prolusions, as they were commonly called, have survived, but among those few are some of Milton's.

Now among Milton's prolusions is one supporting the contention that day is more excellent than night; and it contains passages so like passages in *L'Allegro* that the two compositions must be connected. Further, Milton in his prolusion, near the beginning, said that the topic was better suited to a poetical exercise than to a contest of oratory. I have little doubt that *L'Allegro*, as well as describing the activities of the cheerful man, is his poetical exercise on the superiority of day over night, the poetical counterpart of his prolusion; and that *Il Penseroso* is his poetical exercise on the superiority of night over day, the poetical counterpart of the prolusion he might have written if he had been called on, not to defend, but to oppose the appointed thesis. I have little doubt too that Milton wrote the two poems during his later years at Cambridge, and that he read them to an undergraduate audience or at least passed them to his undergraduate friends in manuscript.

It takes very little observation of the poems to see how faithfully they pursue the themes of day and light or night and darkness respectively, and with carefully contrasted correspondences. Melancholy, which Milton begins *L'Allegro* by attacking and banishing, is kin to blackest midnight; Mirth, in whose praise he writes, is daughter of the dawn of day. Both poems have a plot which consists in a simple progression of time. The plot of *L'Allegro* begins with daybreak, when the lark startles the night and the cock scatters the last remains of darkness as a victorious army routs the stragglers of a defeated enemy. The sun, great source of daylight, appears in regal splendour. The cheerful man then shares in, or watches, activities that fit the various times of day till evening. But even then light is not defeated, and the cheerful man carries his cheerfulness into night's hostile realms by resorting to artificial light. He enters the festivities of the town, where Hymen carries his taper and mask and pageantry suggests the light of many candles. *Il Penseroso* follows the same pattern, only with night and darkness substituted for light and day. It begins by attacking the sun, great source of light: the sun is vain, merely serving to show the foolish motes that play in its beams. The plot begins in the evening, when the nightingale begins to sing. Moonlight replaces the garishness of sunlight, and the firelight indoors consists of mere embers that are as gloomy as they are light. The thoughtful man watches and meditates all night and, when dawn comes, he carries his meditations into the hostile realms of day, seeking the dimness of shades or the subdued light of cathedral or cloister.

The metre of *L'Allegro* and *Il Penseroso*, often called the octosyllabic couplet, because the usual line (though not necessarily all lines) is one of eight syllables and the rhymes come in pairs, was rather rare in Milton's day, but had been widely used in the Middle Ages. Shakespeare used it incidentally—for instance, in *A Midsummer Night's Dream* and Gower's prologues in *Pericles*—and Milton may have derived it from him. But he may have got it from Gower direct or from the medieval romances themselves or from recent use. A metre with so short a line is apt to grow monotonous; but Milton escapes monotony by keeping his poems short, and by his instinct to vary the type of line without breaking the rhythmical pattern that gives the metre its character. This pattern is that of four short-long or iambic feet, as in the line:

> Was never heard the nymphs to daunt.

Here are four very definite iambic feet, with no doubt about the stresses. But Milton never puts two such lines together. The line before is,

> Where the rude axe with heavèd stroke,

which consists of a trochee, or long-short, a spondee, or long-long, followed by two iambs. And the line after is,

> Or fright them from their hallowed haunt,

where, though there may be nominally four iambs, the second, 'them from' is so divided up in the actual reading and so faintly stressed on the second syllable that it gives a very different effect from the line before. Sometimes Milton slips in extra syllables, as in,

> To many a youth and many a maid,

where there are ten instead of the usual eight. I do not mean that Milton planned these metrical effects or thought in terms of feet or syllables. In the heat and stress of composition, of forcing words into an expressive shape, the poet can only follow his instincts; and Milton's instinct, since he had much to say, was to vary the metre he was using.

What is Milton trying to say in *L'Allegro* and *Il Penseroso*? To limit our answer to the twin attempts to describe the respective activities of the cheerful and thoughtful man and the respective merits of day and night would be unhelpful and needlessly timid. It certainly helps us to know that the poems are a kind of debate, just as it helps us to grasp the plot of a novel. But you have only to reflect what different things different writers have made of the same plot to see that there should be more to say.

The principal and most general thing Milton has to express is happiness, and not a passive but an active happiness, and further a happiness about many different things. Milton does not describe cheerfulness and melancholy, day and night, as alternatives; he believes you can enjoy them all. If he had believed otherwise he would have made us feel a conflict; and that is the very thing he does not do. On the contrary he is serene and assured; the thrust and yet the liquid flow of the verse tells us this. Why should Milton have been so happy? There may have been the special reason that, after a time when things had gone wrong, he was enjoying life at college, where his character and talents were at last being appreciated. This is uncertain, but we are on safer ground if we conjecture that Milton's happiness had something to do with the state of England when he wrote. Milton probably wrote these poems in 1631, and in 1639 civil war began with Charles's first attempt to invade Scotland. It is very difficult for us not to cast the shadow of the civil war backward; but England of 1631 was no more certain that there would be civil war in eight years than England of 1906 was certain there would be a world war after the same interval. At both dates there were disturbing events: ecclesiastical quarrels in 1631, and the growing threat of the German Navy in 1906. But these disturbing events were trivial compared with the actualities, unknown and scarcely feared by then, of subsequent disaster. There were many things in the England of 1631 that would revolt or terrify us: the cruelty to criminals, to lunatics, to animals, the prevalence of the plague. But there were many things we could envy. There was a healthy balance between town and country. Classes, though distinct, had more common ground and were separated by milder extremes of wealth or poverty than later; and there were good chances of passing from one class to another. There had been civil peace since the battle of Bosworth, and, though there was strife within the Church, unity was not yet lost. Milton, the puritan, was just as much a member of the Church of England as the High Church Archbishop Laud. The universities were flourishing, and the standard of learning in the country was high; yet the country-folk still cherished their fairy superstitions. Whatever Milton's private sources of happiness in 1631, something of the richness and balance of English life at that date has got into his poems.

III. "On the Morning of Christ's Nativity"

IF *L'Allegro* and *Il Penseroso* are poems written in an old-established traditional metre and pervaded by a strong social sense, the *Nativity Ode*, written near Christmas 1629, probably about a year and a half earlier, is original and individual in its verse and in its tone. In some ways it is indeed very much of its age. Religious subjects were then common, and some of the notions which struck later generations as extravagant or grotesque were quite in keeping with the poetical habits of the time. At the beginning of the hymn Milton puts the wintry weather prevalent at the time of Christ's birth in terms of the earth, pictured as a living creature, begging the air to clothe her imperfections with a mantle of snow; and we are to assume that the air consented to the request. Later the sun and the rosy clouds of sunrise are pictured as a man waking up in a four-poster bed with red hangings. These notions were quite in accord with contemporary taste, and fix the poem to its age. But beyond them the metre, with its highly pronounced character, is Milton's own invention; and the mood of the poem is personal to Milton at the time. Not that it is purely personal, but the personal element combines with the more public to complicate the poem, a complication to which the unusual metre is appropriate and which makes the *Nativity Ode* more difficult than *L'Allegro* and *Il Penseroso*.

We happen to know something of the conditions in which Milton wrote the *Nativity Ode* from one of his Latin poems, the sixth elegy. There he speaks of the discipline to which the writer of the highest types of poetry must submit himself, and in so doing he makes it plain that round this time he dedicated himself to poetry. Such a dedication is not unique. Wordsworth recounts his in the *Prelude*, and Keats in his early poem, *Sleep and Poetry*. Now there is something both youthfully exuberant and very solemn about the metre and the content of Milton's ode. The stanza Milton invented is both lilting and reverberant, while he combines childlike simplicity:

> The shepherds on the lawn
> Or ere the point of dawn
> Sat simply chatting in a rustic row;

and picturesque exuberance:

> With radiant feet the tissued clouds down steering

with direct and tremendous sonority:

> The wakeful trump of doom must thunder through the deep.

And I believe these qualities to answer that mixture of feeling Milton must have experienced when he made his decision: the vitality of youthful excitement at having undertaken a great enterprise, and a sense of awe because the enterprise itself was so solemn and so responsible: responsible, because in Milton's day the poet was looked on as a teacher, and the epic poet as a teacher on a level with the great prophets. Even if I am not right in seeing just this kind of feeling in the *Ode* there is no doubt that it expresses generally the spring and excitement of healthy youth, and wonder at the variety and awe-inspiring hazards of life. It expresses the kind of feeling any lively and sensitive and serious young man is apt to have in entering an enterprise on which he sets a very high value. But I still think the personal feeling is there also, and that when in the last stanza of the introduction Milton bids the heavenly Muse present his poem to the infant Christ he is looking on that poem as the first fruits of his new-dedicated poetic gift.

It is easier to feel the effect of the wonderful stanza Milton invented for the *Nativity Ode* than to describe how he got that effect. But at least it should be plain that he works through two contrasts. The first six lines make a metrical unit within which there is the contrast between four short lines of three feet and two longer lines of five feet; and this alternation provokes and excites. But Milton proceeds to allay the reader's excitement, and smooth out and solemnize his feelings by a second and contrasted rhythmical unit, a rhymed couplet. But it is a peculiar couplet, and not the familiar kind with which Shakespeare ends his sonnets or Chaucer his poems in the seven-line stanza known as 'rime royal,' the even couplet of two five-stressed lines. Milton's couplet has four stresses in the first and six in the second line, and in so having produces a powerful and unexpected effect. Although not in itself weighty, the four-stress or octosyllabic iambic line, which is the first of the final couplet, falls with great dignity and calm assurance in its context; and the reason is that having just had two series of two short lines followed by a long one we now expect still another short line of three stresses, and find a line containing one more stress to be unexpectedly long and emphatic, and thus reassuring. The long line of six stresses, technically called an alexandrine, adds final breadth and majesty to the existing repose and assurance. Once again, it must not be thought that Milton composed his stanza in any deliberate way, or that he thought in terms of lines of this or that length. He wrote as he did because he sought the metrical rendering of the feeling which animated him at the time. Nevertheless it may interest the *reader* to see how the metre Milton chose did in fact produce the effect he desired.

It often happens that a great metrical invention is taken up and used by later poets. The 'rime royal' Chaucer introduced and the *Fairy Queen* stanza Spenser introduced into England have a long history in English literature. As far as I know only one English poet imitated Milton's *Nativity Ode* stanza, and then only in such a way as to recall the original poem. In his drama *Hellas* Shelley has a chorus describing world revolutions in general and the Christian revolution in particular, and in each of his three stanzas he

introduces sets of lines that plainly imitate the opening six
lines in Milton's stanza. Here is the last verse, where the
words as well as the rhythm recall very plainly certain lines
of Milton's poem. The lines where the imitation occurs
are printed in italics.

> Swift as the radiant shapes of sleep
>   From one whose dreams are Paradise
> Fly, when the fond wretch wakes to weep,
>   And Day peers forth with her blank eyes;
>   *So fleet, so faint, so fair,*
>   *The Powers of earth and air*
> *Fled from the folding-star of Bethlehem:*
>   *Apollo, Pan, and Love,*
>   *And even Olympian Jove*
> *Grew weak, for killing Truth had glared on them;*
>   *Our hills and seas and streams,*
>   *Dispeopled of their dreams,*
> *Their waters turned to blood, their dew to tears,*
>   *Wailed for the golden years.*

And this imitation, plain though it is, does not extend
beyond a part of Milton's stanza, which as a whole has
remained uncopied.

IV. "Arcades" and "Comus"

MILTON left Cambridge in the summer of 1632, at the age
of twenty-three. Instead of entering a profession he went
to live with his parents at the village of Horton near Coln-
brook in Buckinghamshire. He remained there till, nearly
six years later, he made a journey to the Continent to finish
his education. We know that he used his time at Horton
in following the studies which his age thought essential for
anyone aspiring to be a writer of the highest type of poetry,
the epic. He studied, among other things, world history

from the original authorities. Horton was within easy reach of London, and Milton used to make frequent journeys there, particularly to find the latest books on mathematics (a rapidly developing science just then), and music. Milton's younger brother, Christopher, was a law student of the Inner Temple at this time; and it may be through him that Milton was tempted to try his hand at the literary form of the masque in his two next poems included in this selection, *Arcades* and *Comus*. Not long after Milton moved to Horton the Inns of Court combined to entertain the King and Queen with a very lavish show, a masque called the *Triumph of Peace*; and it is probable that he heard about the affair from his brother. But the invitations Milton must have received to write the words of *Arcades* and *Comus* were probably procured by his friend, the musician, Henry Lawes. We know for certain that Lawes wrote the music for *Comus*, and that he took the part of the Attendant Spirit. It is highly probable that Lawes wrote the music for *Arcades* and took the part of Genius of the Wood. We know further that Lawes had written part of the music for the *Triumph of Peace*, and all the music for another famous masque produced a few days after, *Cælum Britannicum*, the words of which were by Carew. Whether through his brother, or through his interest in music, Milton got to know Lawes, and Lawes recommended Milton to the aristocratic circles that sponsored *Arcades* and *Comus*.

The masque is an art form most typical of the Elizabethan and early Stuart Ages, ministering to the prevailing love of pageantry and procession. It was an entertainment composed of the elements of poetry, music, procession, dance, and scenic effect; and it employed the talents of poet, composer, choreographer, and architect. For *Cælum Britannicum* Carew, a considerable poet, wrote the words, Henry Lawes, a leading musical composer, wrote the music,

and Inigo Jones, the age's greatest architect, invented the
setting. The masque usually was performed indoors, and
by the aristocracy for an aristocratic audience. In the days
of Milton's youth and early manhood entertainment was
very much more an amateur affair than it is now. We can
get some idea of it by thinking of the game of charades
that still survives precariously, and imagining it immensely
more popular and skilfully played, and reinforced by
music and scenery. The actors in the *Triumph of Peace* were
all amateurs, members of the Inns of Court; those of *Cælum
Britannicum* were the King himself and four young noblemen, among them the two boys who played the brothers
in Milton's *Comus*.

The plot of the masque was usually very slight indeed,
just sufficient to give coherence to the incidental songs and
dances; it counted for just about as much as the plot of a
Gilbert and Sullivan opera. Milton followed this fashion
in *Arcades*, but in *Comus* he enlarged the plot in an entirely
exceptional way.

To understand *Arcades* we must know a little about the
person in whose honour it was written. She was an
aristocratic and distinguished old lady of over seventy, who
had survived two aristocratic and distinguished husbands,
the first the Earl of Derby, and the second Viscount
Brackley. Through her first marriage she was grandmother
of the three children who took the three chief parts in
Comus, and she had eighteen grandchildren in all. She lived
at Harefield in Middlesex, between Uxbridge and Rickmans-
worth. Not very far away, at Ashridge, north of Berk-
hamsted in Hertfordshire (where the Adult Education
College now is), was her son-in-law, the Earl of Bridgewater, with his large family including the three child actors
in *Comus*. We do not know the names of the actors in
Arcades, but they were members of her large family, and

Milton's masque must have been one of several shows got up by this family in honour of this grand survivor from an older generation. When in the first song the Arcadians compare the Countess to Cybele, mother of a hundred gods, Milton is paying her a compliment (exaggerated it is true) on the number and distinction of her descendants.

Though the plot of *Arcades* is slight, it is important for enjoying the poem, just as the setting is important. Masques were usually performed indoors, but it looks as if *Arcades* was a processional masque, performed just outside the house and leading to further entertainment within. We must picture the Countess of Derby seated in state before the front of the house. In the distance appear a band of young people of her family disguised as nymphs and shepherds from pastoral Arcadia. They have heard of the fame of the Countess, so they sing, and now that they see her they find that truth excels report. As they come close the Genius of the Wood, that is of the Harefield estate, stops and addresses them. He knows their mission, their solemn search that has brought them from Arcadia, and he will present them to the Countess. But first he tells them of his duties of tending the woods and plants, thereby paying a compliment to the splendour of the parklands of Harefield. Then as a climax he describes how he listens to the heavenly music of the spheres when he has done, saying that if he could only utter such music himself he might praise his mistress worthily. But he will do his best, and he breaks into the song "O'er the smooth enamelled green" as he leads the Arcadians forward to the presence of the Countess. These reverently salute her, and, full of admiration, sing the beautiful choric song, "Nymphs and Shepherds, dance no more," whose fuller music makes a beautiful contrast with the slighter song of the Genius. In it they advise the other nymphs and shepherds to leave

stony Arcadia for a better soil and Syrinx their queen for
a more princely mistress.

Though short and slight, *Arcades* is beautifully proportioned. The exalted passage about the music of the
spheres makes an apt climax without being so solemn and
heavy as to make the rest seem trivial. In fact, the combination of this exalted and solemn sentiment with the
flexible and delicate lyrics is much like the combination of
these elements in the verse form of the hymn in the *Nativity
Ode*. Like *L'Allegro* and *Il Penseroso*, *Arcades* is a happy
poem, and shows its author content with the England of his
day. Though brought up in the Puritan wing of the Angli-
can Church, he has no quarrel with the cultured and in-
telligent aristocracy for which he is writing, and falls very
readily into the mood of extravagant admiration a poet
was expected to show them.

If *Arcades* was less substantial than the ordinary masque
Comus was very much more so. It is much longer; and the
literary and dramatic parts greatly preponderate over the
dancing and scenic effects. Not that the regular parts are
not all there. One of these was a grotesque set of characters
who performed wild or comic dances; and this performance
was known as the anti-masque. Comus's "rout of monsters,
headed like sundry sorts of wild beasts, but otherwise like
men and women . . . making a riotous and unruly noise"
compose the anti-masque. There are sufficiently elaborate
scenic effects in the changes from the wild wood to Comus's
stately palace and then to Ludlow town and the President's
castle. And there must have been mechanical contrivances
for the descent of the Attendant Spirit at the beginning,
and for the rise and descent of Sabrina. But all these are
subordinated to the literature; and it is not surprising that
the acting version (which has survived in the family for
whom the masque was written) is cut in a few places.

We know a good deal about the circumstances in which *Comus* was produced. Lawes wrote the music, some of which (and it is very beautiful) survives, and he took the part of the Attendant Spirit. We can conjecture that he was stage-manager too, and taught the three children of the Earl of Bridgewater—Lord Brackley, Mr Thomas Egerton, and the Lady Alice Egerton—how to sing or say their lines, for he was already their music-master. It would have been Lawes, too, who commissioned Milton to write the words. We know that the Bridgewater children were young, Lady Alice about fifteen, and the two boys younger; but in an age when boys took the tremendous parts of Shakespeare's Lady Macbeth and Cleopatra or of Webster's Vittoria Corombona we need not be surprised. The masque was performed on Michaelmas Day, September 29, 1634, in the great hall, sixty by thirty feet in size, of Ludlow Castle. As *Arcades* was composed to honour a distinguished old lady *Comus* was composed to honour a special occasion. Some time before the date of the performance the Earl of Bridgewater had been appointed to the high office of Lord President of Wales, an office that brought with it Ludlow Castle as his official residence. It was some time before he moved into the Castle; and *Comus* celebrates his moving in and his real assumption of office.

If *Arcades* seems to have been performed in the open *Comus* was certainly performed indoors by artificial light. We must picture a high stage at one end of the hall where not only is the play performed but the Earl and Countess of Bridgewater are seated so that in the final scene they can be transformed from spectators to a part of the show itself. Not that the indoor setting is essential or necessarily preferable. Since Milton's day *Comus* has often been performed in the open, and in recent years with great success by professionals in Regent's Park, London, as a regular part of their repertory.

Comus is less uniform and not so near perfection as *L'Allegro* and *Il Penseroso*, but it shows a great advance in the variety and the power of its poetry. Milton uses the metre of the two earlier pieces freely, but when he first brings it in, in Comus's first speech (line 111), he varies the four-stress couplet with five-stress couplets.

> We that are of purer fire
> Imitate the starry quire,
> Who in their nightly watchful spheres
> Lead in swift round the months and years.
> The sounds and seas, with all their finny drove,
> Now to the moon in wavering morrice move.

The first four lines are in the metre of *L'Allegro*, but Milton is now attempting thoughts and feelings too large to be confined to it, and when he describes the sea dancing to the attraction of the moon in the fifth and sixth lines he issues into a more solemn rhythm through lines of five stresses. As in *Arcades* there are lyrics for singing, but it is the blank verse, the masque's preponderating metre, that is for Milton the great innovation, and the means of his expressing a wider range of feeling than he had attempted hitherto. Not till Milton wrote *Paradise Lost* and *Paradise Regained* in blank verse did that metre become correct for narrative use. Before that it was used, with very rare exceptions, for the drama alone. And when Milton wrote the blank verse of *Comus* he looked not to his future narrative verse but to the tradition of Elizabethan, Jacobean, and Caroline dramas, still very much alive in his own day. He did not borrow his type of blank verse from any one dramatist, but every now and then *Comus* reminds us of passages in the last plays of Shakespeare, *The Winter's Tale* and *The Tempest*, and in the plays of the dramatist Shirley, who was in the

middle of his dramatic career in the year 1634. Indeed, it
looks as if Milton intended to approximate the masque,
traditionally a stiff and formal and very unrealistic literary
form, to the greater realism of the authentic drama. There
are passages in *Comus* which are admirably dramatic, suggesting action and the language used by men in emergencies.
When Comus first hears the Lady coming he stops the
dance of his rout with:

> Break off, break off, I feel the different pace
> Of some chaste footing near about this ground.
> Run to your shrouds within these brakes and trees;
> Our number may affright.

The lines are perfect in expressing Comus's excitement and
expectation, and his hurry to get his monsters out of the
way. But, by letting the drama into the masque, Milton
made difficulties for himself. Once he had begun he should,
to be consistent, have made the whole masque dramatic.
But that he does not do. He allows longer speeches and
more ornament than is consistent with live, genuine drama.
The Elder Brother's speech on chastity, beginning at line
419, is a lovely piece of poetry and admirably suited to
recitation, but its very virtues make us forget the action;
and action is the soul of drama. For ornament take the
Lady's first speech. This begins most dramatically:

> This way the noise was, if mine ear be true,
> My best guide now;

where the monosyllables, breaking the rhythm into small
pieces, suggest the hesitating gait of some one groping her
way in the dark. But later, in spite of her predicament and
the agitation it could not fail to produce, she has the
emotional leisure to convey information about the hour
she last saw her brothers in the most exquisitely round-
about embroidered language:

C

They left me then, when the gray-hooded Even,
Like a sad votarist in palmer's weed
Rose from the hindmost wheels of Phœbus' wain.

The lines are lovely, and perfectly suited to the traditional, ceremonious type of masque. But they come a little oddly after the successful drama before. *Comus* has come down to us in slightly different versions, the familiar version printed in this edition being the latest. It would be wrong to complicate a school edition with details of the changes Milton made from one version to another, but there is a general trend in his changes that is worth recording. It is away from drama and realism, and towards the greater remoteness and ceremony that marked the masque. Milton must have realized that he could not dramatize a masque thoroughly; so in his final version he toned down some of the passages that most suggested the rough and tumble of actual life.

Milton then failed to make *Comus* quite a whole. But he created and gave so much that it would be ill mannered and pedantic to complain. One of the best criticisms of *Comus* is the first, contained in a letter written to Milton by Sir Henry Wotton, Provost of Eton, just before Milton's departure for the Continent not quite four years after the masque was written. Wotton speaks of a "certain Doric delicacy in your songs and odes, whereunto I must plainly confess to have seen yet nothing parallel in our language." Wotton's phrase holds good for the whole masque. There is indeed no poetry like Milton's, it is quite individual; and "Doric delicacy" expresses to perfection the mixture of austerity and grace, of male and female qualities, that marks his earlier verse. (The Dorians were the most virile and energetic of the Greek races, and the Dorian mode in music had the same qualities.) There are passages in *Comus* which are not only elegant and lovely and highly musical but solid

and austere and packed close with varied meaning. Here
is one, from the Lady's first speech, and coming after the
highly ornate passage quoted above. It is both realistic
and infinitely suggestive. The Lady arrives at the place
where she believes the sounds of noisy mirth to have come
from, and she says:

> This is the place, as well as I may guess,
> Whence even now the tumult of loud mirth
> Was rife and perfect in my listening ear,
> Yet nought but single darkness do I find.
> What might this be? A thousand fantasies
> Begin to throng into my memory,
> Of calling shapes, and beckoning shadows dire,
> And airy tongues that syllable men's names
> On sands and shores and desert wildernesses.

This is dramatic. It is natural that the Lady, finding the
merry-makers vanished, should think of stories of will-o'-
the-wisps and mysterious voices and enchantments
generally. But the way in which she describes these stories
stirs our imaginations with the utmost power. In his
anthology, *The Spirit of Man*, Robert Bridges printed the
last five lines by themselves, and with strong effect, for they
do compress into their small compass much of the magic
with which Shakespeare invested his enchanted island in
The Tempest. The passage is in the highest degree delicate
and refined, but it is also "Doric" in its actuality and com-
pression and solidity.

I have said that *Comus*, though nominally a masque and
containing the traditional features of the masque, is very
different from all other specimens of this form. Anyone
with the curiosity to test this statement could conveniently
use Ben Jonson's *Pleasure reconciled with Virtue* for this
purpose. Milton had read it, and introduced echoes of it in
Comus, facts which give it an added interest and relevance.
But it is also a typical masque and a noble piece of poetry;

and serves as a norm of what the masque, at its highest, was like. In being unlike *Pleasure reconciled with Virtue, Comus* was being unlike the masque generally. I said further that though Milton let into the masque form a good deal of contemporary drama he did not carry the process through; as a whole *Comus* does not resemble a Caroline stage play. How then are we to think of it? What in fact does it resemble?

The first thing to note is that *Comus* is an allegory as well as a drama. Comus is a live character, but he is also an allegory of intemperance. The Lady is aristocratic and delicately bred, but she is also an allegorical figure of chastity. Comus's rout of monster-headed men are an allegory of human beings degraded through various types of intemperance into the state of beasts. The wood is an allegory of the perplexities of worldly existence; and, as such, one of the most familiar of all allegories. At the beginning of his *Divine Comedy* Dante loses himself in a dark wood—the wood of life's perplexities. Spenser's enchanted forests have the same meaning. Bunyan begins his *Pilgrim's Progress*, his allegory of the Christian life, with, "As I walked through the wilderness of this world . . ." The same notion occurs in the hymn:

> Through each perplexing path of life
> Our wandering footsteps guide.

Even the heath in *King Lear* is an allegorical heath as well as a piece of waste land open to the elements. If the wood and Comus's palace are allegorical, the action is a pilgrimage and an ordeal. The three children are pilgrims; and the Lady undergoes a chastity ordeal, while the Brothers have their faith and courage tested. All these matters, the allegory, the pilgrimage, and the ordeal, separate *Comus* from contemporary drama and ally it with an earlier, medieval tradition: with the knightly ordeal in Malory, with the first

two books of the *Fairy Queen*, where the Red Cross Knight
and Guyon are tested as they perform their pilgrimages,
and with Bunyan's *Pilgrim's Progress*. The chastity ordeal
is also a medieval theme, being found frequently in the
legendary lives of the Saints.

But if *Comus* is in the tradition of medieval Christian
allegory it is also full of classical ornament. Comus himself
is an allegorical figure and a medieval enchanter; but he is
also a classical god with a Greek pedigree, and his monsters
are in the tradition of Circe and her brute-attendants in the
Odyssey. When the Elder Brother talks of chastity he
reveals a thorough classical education and a knowledge of
Plato, while the Attendant Spirit lives in a realm whose
parts are described in terms of classical mythology. Yet
this classicism is *ornament*, not part of the structure; and it
is like the classical figures you sometimes find added to
very late examples of Gothic architecture—for instance,
Bishop West's chapel in Ely Cathedral. Indeed, the classicism of *Comus* is less important than yet another ingredient
—the magical. As well as being a medieval allegory *Comus*
is a fairy-tale. Fairy-tales are full of ordeals, where the
precise procedure is laid down, and where the least slip
leads to disaster. If the Lady should forget herself for a
moment she is lost, and Comus knows it when in his final
effort to make her drink he says:

> . . . one sip of this
> Will bathe the drooping spirits in delight
> Beyond the bliss of dreams.

If a drink is not magical quantity counts. But of a magical
drink a sip is as potent as a gallon. And if Comus is the base
magician, Sabrina is a form of the good fairy who intervenes
on special occasions. The Attendant Spirit, too, belongs
partly to the world of magic. He is primarily Christian, the
guardian angel; but that does not prevent him from being

also the good spirit, who is present at the birth of the Prince, and does not cease to look after his interests.

This business of the fairy-tale matters greatly because through it you can best enter the world of *Comus*. At bottom we are all drawn to enchanted ground; and we should use that attraction to enjoy *Comus*. Through using it initially we shall perceive the other things *Comus* has to offer. The many bits of drama and real life will show up all the more startlingly in the fairy setting, as when the Elder Brother in his first speech, after speaking remotely about the darkness, suddenly talks of a candle shining from a cottage window with its "long levelled rule of streaming light." That is real life, first-hand observation, and it startles the more for occurring where it does. Similarly sincerely austere morality, the sense of the loveliness of a pure and ordered life, show up the more vividly for the romantic circumstances in which they are set.

V. "Lycidas"

Lycidas is by far the most difficult poem in this volume, but its difficulties are not on the surface as at first sight might be thought, but in the core. Superficially the form of pastoral elegy in which *Lycidas* is cast is for most modern schoolboys remote, unnecessary, and even repellent. To former generations, bred on the classics, this was not so. Virgil's pastorals were taken for granted as quite early reading; and a boy might easily know some of the other great pastoral poems before reading *Lycidas*. Shelley found it natural to write *Adonais*, his elegy on Keats, and Arnold to write *Thyrsis*, his elegy on Clough, in pastoral form. But now most schoolboys are likely to gain their first acquaintance with the pastoral convention through *Lycidas* itself. I do not think they need be put off by the novelty if they think of other artistic conventions quite as violent but easy to accept because widely familiar. Take the opera. It is quite as violent and unnatural a convention to make the characters in a realistic drama sing instead of speak their words as to pretend that ordinary people are shepherds feeding their flocks. The most rigidly conventional modern literary form is that of the detective story. A man from another age encountering this form for the first time would be greatly bewildered. Why, he might ask, the pretence of constant murder in a country where violent crime is not especially common, and why the recurrent theme of the least likely person being ultimately the criminal? But if he was told at once that these things were all part of a game he would soon acquire the right mood. Just so the pastoral elegy was a kind of game, which authors agreed to play according to certain rules. It was part of the game, for instance, that certain people should come to lament the body or the death of the elegy's subject. Once you realize that the rules of this game, as of other games, should be accepted and entirely allowed, and that what matters is the way the game is played, you will have no initial difficulty with the conventions, queer indeed in themselves, of *Lycidas*.

Three years separate *Comus* and *Lycidas*. Like *Comus*, *Lycidas* was written on request for a special occasion; and, just as Milton took liberties with the masque form, so he turned to his own uses the form of pastoral elegy he chose for commemorating the death by drowning of his friend Edward King. *Lycidas* is a more complicated poem than *Comus* in that it includes more kinds of feeling, and we can be sure that in the interval between them Milton had matured rapidly. Not that you cannot take *Lycidas* simply.

It is what it professes to be, an elegy on King; there is
nothing in it that cannot be related to him. King had
written verses, and was destined for the Church. It was
appropriate therefore that Milton should talk of poetic
fame and introduce St Peter, one of the supreme Christian
pastors. The description of King in heaven is the natural
ending of a Christian elegy. But it would be wrong to
think of *Lycidas* as no more than a fundamentally simple
elegy made to look elaborate by its pastoral form and much
added ornament.

One complication that becomes plain when you look
close at *Lycidas* is that the poem is about Milton himself as
much as about Edward King. And if the reader remembers
the conditions in which Milton wrote he will understand
that the cases of Milton and his dead friend were in some
ways very similar. Milton wrote *Lycidas* not long before
he began a continental journey, which was to have included
Greece as well as Italy in its scope. Whether the poem's
last line—

> To-morrow to fresh woods and pastures new

—refers to this future journey is uncertain; but when
writing *Lycidas* Milton must have had this journey in mind.
As King had attempted a journey to Ireland so Milton was
about to attempt a longer and in itself more perilous one.
He could hardly escape the comparison. Moreover, there
were similarities apart from their voyages. The two had
been at the same college in the same university. They shared
an interest in poetry; both had at one time been destined for
the Church. How could Milton have escaped the thought
that he might well make the analogy complete, when he
came to undertake his journey, by dying likewise? That
Milton did in fact have some such thoughts is clear from
his reference in the second paragraph to his own "destined

urn" and "sable shroud." As a reason for writing on
Lycidas he says:

> So may some gentle Muse
> With lucky words favour my destined urn,
> And as he passes turn
> And bid fair peace be to my sable shroud;
> For we were nursed upon the selfsame hill,
> Fed the same flock by fountain, shade, and rill.

This means, "If I die some one will requite me with a
memorial elegy, for in other ways the resemblance between
King and myself is complete." Nor was Milton's thought
of possible death unreasonable. There had been the plague
in England about this time, and it had touched Milton's
home village of Horton, while a sea-voyage was dangerous
in those days—in the Mediterranean not only from weather
but from pirates—in a way we can hardly conceive of to-
day. And when in lines 64–76 Milton speaks of intense
labour, the ambition to see the fruits of it, and the tragedy
of death intervening before those fruits have been produced, he is really being more apt to his own case than to that
of King. Milton has staked everything on a great poem,
prolonging his education and wearing himself out with
unremitting labour to be capable of it; and the thought, as
the project grew nearer fulfilment, that all this labour
might be for nothing must have been difficult to bear.
The "abhorred shears" had a peculiarly harrowing personal application.

But *Lycidas* is much more than the record first of grief
for a dead friend and second of harrowing personal feelings.
It recounts how turbulent and painful feelings are resolved
into a new mood of serene resolution. And, though Milton
in a way speaks for himself, the kind of experience he describes applies to every human being, and the poem in the end
gets quite away from the personal into the universally true.

Now the difficulty of *Lycidas* is that Milton does not *state* any of these things. Instead he recounts various imaginary happenings, and we can reach the core of the poem only by inference from these happenings. The best poetry usually works in this way: not by direct statement of moral truths or universal commonplaces; but by creating situations or actions or characters which somehow imply or force us to infer these truths or commonplaces.

It is a usual experience in reading good poetry that the very thing that is initially most difficult or baffling or repellent ends by giving the most enlightenment. Let the reader remember this when he tackles *Lycidas*. At first sight nothing could be more discouraging than the length and the apparently needless elaboration with which Milton in the first few lines complains that he is not ready to write more poetry, that he does not want to write, but that he cannot escape his obligation to commemorate his friend. The sentiment is extremely simple, and yet the poet must needs go out of his way to express it in uneasy rhythms and with elaborate classical circumlocution. On the face of it the opening is vilely pretentious. To be assured that Milton knew what he was doing I advise the reader to turn straight to the final paragraph. There you have (granted the pastoral convention) the utmost clarity of statement, simple language, and serenely assured rhythms. Put the two passages together, and you will easily see that the whole point of the poem is the change from one mood to another; from a mood of turbulence, almost despair, to one of serene, well-grounded resolution. The body of the poem in between deals with both moods, and the way one supplants the other. I will now go on to describe how I think the poem develops.

Lycidas falls into six main sections: a prologue, four main sections, and an epilogue. The prologue, consisting of ll. 1–24, gives Milton's reason for writing an elegy on King, and introduces the simultaneous theme of his own possible death. The uneasiness of the rhythm forecasts the uneasy or bitter sentiments of the two following sections. The second section, ll. 25–84, speaks of the life common to Lycidas and the poet, laments that the Muse could not protect her own son, Lycidas, turns to Milton's own troubles at this time, his fears lest he may die before his great work for which he has sacrificed so much is complete, and leads up to the larger topic of fame as the reward of good deeds on this earth. Why should a man take an infinity of pains when it may be all for nothing? Surely there is an injustice in the world when, as Wordsworth put it,

> . . . the good die first,
> And they whose hearts are dry as summer dust
> Burn to the socket.

A voice from heaven asserts that it is in heaven not on earth that fame requites good deeds. But by some lowering of the rhythmic tension Milton robs the heavenly assertion of ultimate convincingness. His sense of injustice on earth is not really appeased. It *should* be appeased, but it is not. And we are not surprised when the third section, ll. 85–131, resumes the theme of injustice on earth. The burden of this section is a series of complaints at Lycidas's death and the ills of time, culminating in St Peter's terrifying denunciation of the corrupt clergy and prophecy of their ultimate fate. In these second and third sections Milton stated with immense passion and power some of the things in life that distressed him. And after such a statement we expect some conclusion, whether optimistic after all or despairing or stoical. But, instead of answering our expectations, Milton takes our breath away by one of the most sudden changes in literature. After the vague but overwhelming terror of the "two-handed engine," he begins his fourth section with the unruffled gentleness of "Return, Alpheus," and the rest. This section extends from l. 132 to 164, and it is an escape from intolerable reality into a lovely world of make-believe. Such an escape is indeed some kind of a solution of the difficulties of a hard world, and in suggesting it Milton greatly enlarges the scope of his poem. But he does not really contemplate anything so easy and ignoble. He knows that the surmise with which he dallies is false; and, though we enjoy the miraculous journey—he takes us among the flowers and to the depths of the sea—we know that the true solution of his troubles remains to be presented. The fifth section, ll. 165–185, though overtly describing Lycidas in heaven, does much more. When Milton tells the shepherds to weep no more he means not only that Lycidas does not need our tears but that he himself has acquired the courage to meet and triumph over the ills he has described. And the ecstatic comparison of the resurrected Lycidas in heaven to the sun which

> Flames in the forehead of the morning sky

after its evening eclipse expresses the possibility of a new life that may spring out of the depths of tragedy. The last section, l. 186 to the end, so calm and so assured and yet so intense, fixes the mood of resolution that has succeeded the mood of trouble, or despair. The poet is ready to face anything life has to offer him.

Such is the trend of *Lycidas*. Its meaning distils itself into a matter of belief shared by all the great religions: that means count for more than ends, and results count for less than personal integrity, that by renouncing the state of mind where results come first you acquire a new or regenerate state of mind better able to meet life's problems.

I must repeat that *Lycidas* is a difficult poem, and must grant that some readers will think I find in it more than is there. Indeed, there must be a good many people who, even after giving *Lycidas* a good chance, will frankly feel coldly about it, and about other poetry of similar difficulty and elusiveness. Or they may succeed in enjoying some of the details, but not in grasping the whole. It is most important that such readers should not thereby be put off all poetry, for there is abundant poetry of other kinds calling for different powers of appreciation. On the other hand, there are strong reasons for persisting with *Lycidas*. George Borrow in one of his novels describes how his first experience of horsemanship was on a powerful and spirited Suffolk cob. The cob led him a dance of miles across country, but somehow he stuck on its back. In the end cob and rider reached home, the rider sweating in every pore and aching in every limb, but triumphant, and knowing that he now had the freedom of the whole tribe of horses. Just so a reader who has mastered *Lycidas* will have obtained the freedom of a whole kingdom of literature.

VI. Sonnets

WITHIN the sonnet form there are certain technical differences of rhyme and paragraph; these are touched on in the notes. But there are two very different ways in which the sonnet as a whole can be disposed. There is the sonnet sequence, and there is the detached sonnet. The sequence is a series of sonnets on a single subject, like Spenser's *Amoretti* written in praise of his future wife or Wordsworth's on the river Duddon. The detached sonnet deals with a self-sufficient thought or comments on a single person or a topical event.

Milton's sonnets are entirely of the second kind, and they

are all personal and topical. Even the most apparently generalized of them, that to the nightingale, refers to the spring of a particular year. He laments that in earlier years it has been the ill-omened cuckoo he has heard first, and begs the nightingale *this year* to favour him with early song. The rest are most obviously occasional, *When the Assault was intended to the City* or *On his Blindness*; or personal, *To Mr H. Lawes, on his Airs* or *To Mr Lawrence*. Rossetti called the sonnet "a moment's monument," and that phrase suits Milton's sonnets very well: they treat of a present theme, and yet in their firmness and dignity they are monumental.

Milton learnt Italian early, possibly while still at school, and through the prompting of his chief school-friend, Diodati, the son of Italian parents. And it was probably through reading recent Italian sonnets that he was led to forsake the sonnet sequence favoured by the Elizabethans and to write topical sonnets. He wrote the two earliest sonnets in this volume, *To the Nightingale* and *On his being arrived at the Age of Twenty-three*, along with a number of sonnets in Italian. The other English sonnets all belong to the period of his life between his return from Italy and his beginning on *Paradise Lost*, in fact to the period when he wrote nearly all his prose, and when he was mixed up in contemporary politics or was the servant of the Commonwealth. Unable to give his mind to sustained poetical composition he was able to satisfy some of his poetical urge by these occasional pieces. It was not all loss that Milton was forced to postpone his great poem so long. Compared with *Paradise Lost* and *Samson Agonistes*, the sonnets are small affairs; yet through being forced into so small a literary form Milton expressed sides of his mind that otherwise might have remained hidden. We might have missed the delicate tenderness with which he commemorates his second wife or the elegance of his invitation to Lawrence to spend a social evening with him. If you read *Paradise Lost* closely you will see that tenderness and elegance are not absent; but you are very likely to miss them there unless you begin with expecting them on account of their presence in the sonnets.

Milton belonged to a literary tradition that thought modern literature should do in its own way the kind of thing that the Greeks and Romans had done so well in theirs. In writing his sonnets, though he derived his verse form from the Italians, he clearly thought that he was recalling the odes of Horace. These odes take their subjects from actual events and people, and their range is from the high political—the death of Cleopatra for instance—to the trivial. Strengthened by this Horatian precedent, Milton could vary the subjects of his sonnets from the fierce political protest *On the Late Massacre in Piemont* to quiet advice to Cyriac Skinner to relax and be cheerful when the chance comes along. In itself Milton's regard of Horace is of small importance; what matters is that through that regard Milton was encouraged to be topical and easy rather than rapturously abstracted, and to tell us things about himself he might easily have not thought worth telling.

VII. A Note on the Frontispiece

THE frontispiece shows a painting in the National Gallery of Art, Washington, by the Italian painter, Tiepolo. He lived later than Milton, 1693–1770, but he worked in exactly the same classical tradition, and can aptly be compared to him. The painting presents the legend of Apollo and Daphne, as recounted by Ovid. Apollo, the sun-god, loved

Daphne, daughter of the river-god Peneus and of Earth,
but she refused his advances and ran away from him.
Apollo pursued, and, as he was about to catch her, she
called on her father and mother for help, and they baffled
Apollo by turning her into a laurel. In the picture Apollo,
with the sun-halo round his head, runs towards Daphne
from the right. Daphne herself is in process of transformation. One leg has already turned into a tree-trunk
firmly rooted in the ground, while her hands, which she
holds up in alarm, have their fingers sprouting into laurel-
shoots. Below her is her father, Peneus, with the proper
attributes of a personified river. He wears a crown of
sedge; he leans on an urn out of which water flows, and
before him is the kind of oar that served for a rudder.
Behind, on the left in the shadows, is Cupid. The shadows
and his mournful expression of face betoken the unhappy
end of the romance he had been promoting.

Tiepolo's picture may help the reader of Milton for two
reasons.

First, there are things in Milton which it illustrates very
aptly. They are things that may seem strange nowadays,
but when we see them recurring in the work of a painter
in another country, who had never read Milton, we can
understand that in an earlier age they were quite natural.
The legend itself of Apollo and Daphne is strange, but
Tiepolo did not hesitate to make a picture of it, and Milton
referred to it as something well known in the passage I have
already discussed, where Comus has the Lady a prisoner in
his magic chair and tells her not to move, for with a wave
of his wand he can make her like Daphne, "root-bound,
that fled Apollo." Tiepolo's picture illustrates Milton's
"root-bound" to perfection. Another matter common to
Milton and Tiepolo is their showing brooks and rivers in
the guise of persons. Tiepolo's river-god, Peneus, is a

completely human figure, realistically drawn. Even so in *Comus* Milton introduces the river Severn as a woman, Sabrina. But closest to Tiepolo's Peneus is Milton's Camus, personification of the river Cam. Camus was old like Peneus, a "reverend sire"; and his "bonnet," like that of Peneus, was of sedge.

Second, these details are a part of a larger habit of relying on classical legend to present or to illustrate a human situation. And again the picture may help the reader to understand that this habit of reliance was natural to Milton and his contemporaries. And it was not only natural but it was bound up with a set of assumptions common in the ages of Milton and Tiepolo, and derived partly from Greece and Rome; assumptions about the natural dignity of man and his noble possibilities if he acts well. Such an assumption underlies *Comus* with its ardent-minded characters, and it underlies the grand proportions of Tiepolo's figures. There are many natural descriptions in Milton, some ideal, some lifelike, but they are always subordinate to the human interest. There are beautiful pieces of nature in Tiepolo's picture—the water from the urn, the pine on the left, the rocky landscape on the right—but they are all subordinate to the human emotions of the actors.

Classical legend was not the only store of reference that came naturally to Milton and Tiepolo; for another great store was the Bible, and Milton assumes a knowledge of medieval legend too. My point in including this frontispiece is to show that all these items of knowledge Milton used were common property. He used the legend of Daphne and Apollo as he used that of Moses on Mount Sinai, not to parade his learning or to be recondite, but for the very opposite reason, because he knew that his hearers or readers would be familiar with it.

D

VIII. Bibliography

The following books may be found useful for further reading:

Hanford, J. H., *A Milton Handbook* (Bell, 1935).

Macaulay, Rose, *Milton* (Duckworth, 1934).

Pattison, Mark, *John Milton* (Macmillan, 1925).

Raleigh, Walter, *Milton* (Edward Arnold, 1900).

Tillyard, E. M. W., *Milton* (Chatto and Windus, 1930).

Tillyard, E. M. W., *The Miltonic Setting* (Chatto and Windus, 1947).

Tillyard, E. M. W., *Studies in Milton* (Chatto and Windus, 1951).

Warner, Rex, *John Milton* (Max Parrish, 1950).

ON THE MORNING OF CHRIST'S NATIVITY

I

This is the month and this the happy morn
Wherein the Son of Heaven's eternal King,
Of wedded maid and virgin mother born,
Our great redemption from above did bring;
For so the holy sages once did sing   5
That he our deadly forfeit should release
And with his Father work us a perpetual peace.

II

That glorious form, that light insufferable,
And that far-beaming blaze of majesty,
Wherewith he wont at Heaven's high council-
    table   10
To sit the midst of Trinal Unity,
He laid aside; and, here with us to be,
Forsook the courts of everlasting day,
And chose with us a darksome house of mortal clay.

III

Say, Heavenly Muse, shall not thy sacred vein   15
Afford a present to the Infant God?
Hast thou no verse, no hymn, or solemn strain
To welcome him to this his new abode,
Now while the heaven, by the Sun's team untrod,
Hath took no print of the approaching light,   20
And all the sprangled host keep watch in squadrons
    bright?

IV

See how from far upon the eastern road
The star-led wizards haste with odours sweet;
O run, prevent them with thy humble ode,
And lay it lowly at his blessed feet!   25
Have thou the honour first thy Lord to greet,
And join thy voice unto the angel quire,
From out his secret altar touched with hallowed fire.

THE HYMN

I

It was the winter wild,
While the Heaven-born Child   30
    All meanly wrapped in the rude manger lies;
Nature in awe to him
Had doffed her gaudy trim,
    With her great Master so to sympathize:
It was no season then for her   35
To wanton with the sun, her lusty paramour.

II

Only with speeches fair
She woos the gentle air
    To hide her guilty front with innocent snow
And on her naked shame,   40
Pollute with sinful blame,
    The saintly veil of maiden white to throw:
Confounded, that her Maker's eyes
Should look so near upon her foul deformities.

III

But he, her fears to cease,   45
Sent down the meek-eyed Peace;

She, crowned with olive green, came softly sliding
Down through the turning sphere,
His ready harbinger,
    With turtle wing the amorous clouds dividing;   50
And waving wide her myrtle wand
She strikes a universal peace through sea and land.

IV

No war or battle's sound
Was heard the world around:
    The idle spear and shield were high uphung,   55
The hookèd chariot stood
Unstained with hostile blood,
    The trumpet spake not to the armèd throng;
And kings sat still with awful eye
As if they surely knew their sovran Lord was by.   60

V

But peaceful was the night
Wherein the Prince of Light
  His reign of peace upon the earth began:
The winds with wonder whist
Smoothly the waters kissed,   65
    Whispering new joys to the mild ocean,
Who now hath quite forgot to rave,
While birds of calm sit brooding on the charmèd wave.

VI

The stars with deep amaze
Stand fixed in steadfast gaze,   70
    Bending one way their precious influence,
And will not take their flight
For all the morning light
    Or Lucifer that often warned them thence;
But in their glimmering orbs did glow   75
Until their Lord himself bespake and bid them go.

VII

And though the shady gloom
Had given day her room,
   The sun himself withheld his wonted speed,
And hid his head for shame   80
As his inferior flame
   The new-enlightened world no more should need:
He saw a greater Sun appear
Than his bright throne or burning axletree could bear.

VIII

The shepherds on the lawn,   85
Or ere the point of dawn,
   Sat simply chatting in a rustic row;
Full little thought they than
That the mighty Pan
   Was kindly come to live with them below;   90
Perhaps their loves, or else their sheep,
Was all that did their silly thoughts so busy keep.

IX

When such music sweet
Their hearts and ears did greet
   As never was by mortal finger strook,   95
Divinely-warbled voice
Answering the stringèd noise,
   As all their souls in blissful rapture took:
The air, such pleasure loth to lose,
With thousand echoes still prolongs each heavenly
    close.   100

X

Nature, that heard such sound
Beneath the hollow round
   Of Cynthia's seat the airy region thrilling,

Now was almost won
To think her part was done   105
   And that her reign had here its last fulfilling;
She knew such harmony alone
Could hold all heaven and earth in happier union.

XI

At last surrounds their sight
A globe of circular light   110
   That with long beams the shamefaced Night arrayed;
The helmèd Cherubim
And sworded Seraphim
   Are seen in glittering ranks with wings displayed,
Harping in loud and solemn quire,   115
With unexpressive notes, to Heaven's new-born Heir.

XII

Such music as 'tis said
Before was never made
   But when of old the Sons of Morning sung,
While the Creator great   120
His constellations set
   And the well-balanced world on hinges hung,
And cast the dark foundations deep
And bid the weltering waves their oozy channel keep.

XIII

Ring out, ye crystal spheres,   125
Once bless our human ears,
   (If ye have power to touch our senses so),
And let your silver chime
Move in melodious time,
   And let the bass of heaven's deep organ blow;   130
And with your ninefold harmony
Make up full consort to the angelic symphony.

XIV

For if such holy song
Enwrap our fancy long,
 Time will run back and fetch the Age of Gold; 135
And speckled Vanity
Will sicken soon and die,
 And leprous Sin will melt from earthly mould;
And Hell itself will pass away
And leave her dolorous mansions to the peering day. 140

XV

Yea, Truth and Justice then
Will down return to men,
 Orbed in a rainbow; and like glories wearing,
Mercy will sit between
Throned in celestial sheen, 145
 With radiant feet the tissued clouds down steering;
And Heaven as at some festival
Will open wide the gates of her high palace-wall.

XVI

But wisest Fate says No,
This must not yet be so; 150
 The babe yet lies in smiling infancy
That on the bitter cross
Must redeem our loss,
 So both himself and us to glorify;
Yet first to those ychained in sleep 155
The wakeful trump of doom must thunder through the
  deep

XVII

With such a horrid clang
As on Mount Sinai rang,
 While the red fire and smouldering clouds outbrake:

The aged Earth aghast   160
With terror of that blast
   Shall from the surface to the centre shake,
When at the world's last session
The dreadful Judge in middle air shall spread his throne.

XVIII

And then at last our bliss   165
Full and perfect is,
   But now begins; for from this happy day
The old Dragon under ground
In straiter limits bound
   Not half so far casts his usurpèd sway,   170
And wroth to see his kingdom fail
Swinges the scaly horror of his folded tail.

XIX

The oracles are dumb,
No voice or hideous hum
   Runs through the archèd roof in words deceiving. 175
Apollo from his shrine
Can no more divine,
   With hollow shriek the steep of Delphos leaving;
No nightly trance or breathèd spell
Inspires the pale-eyed priest from the prophetic cell. 180

XX

The lonely mountains o'er
And the resounding shore,
   A voice of weeping heard and loud lament;
From haunted spring and dale
Edged with poplar pale,   185
   The parting Genius is with sighing sent;
With flower-inwoven tresses torn
The Nymphs in twilight shade of tangled thickets mourn.

XXI

In consecrated earth
And on the holy hearth   190
   The Lars and Lemures moan with midnight plaint;
In urns and altars round
A drear and dying sound
   Affrights the flamens at their service quaint;
And the chill marble seems to sweat,   195
While each peculiar Power forgoes his wonted seat.

XXII

Peor and Baalim
Forsake their temples dim,
   With that twice-battered god of Palestine;
And moonèd Ashtaroth,   200
Heaven's queen and mother both,
   Now sits not girt with tapers' holy shine;
The Lybic Hammon shrinks his horn;
In vain the Tyrian maids their wounded Thammuz
    mourn.

XXIII

And sullen Moloch, fled,   205
Hath left in shadows dread
   His burning idol all of blackest hue;
In vain with cymbals' ring
They call the grisly king,
   In dismal dance about the furnace blue;   210
The brutish gods of Nile as fast,
Isis and Orus and the dog Anubis, haste.

XXIV

Nor is Osiris seen
In Memphian grove or green,
   Trampling the unshowered grass with lowings
    loud;   215

Nor can he be at rest
Within his sacred chest;
   Nought but profoundest hell can be his shroud;
In vain with timbrelled anthems dark
The sable-stolèd sorcerers bear his worshipped ark.   220

XXV

He feels from Juda's land
The dreaded Infant's hand;
   The rays of Bethlehem blind his dusky eyne;
Nor all the gods beside
Longer dare abide,   225
   Not Typhon huge ending in snaky twine:
Our babe, to show his Godhead true,
Can in his swaddling bands control the damnèd crew.

XXVI

So when the sun in bed,
Curtained with cloudy red,   230
   Pillows his chin upon an orient wave,
The flocking shadows pale
Troop to the infernal jail,
   Each fettered ghost slips to his several grave,
And the yellow-skirted fays   235
Fly after the night-steeds, leaving their moon-loved
    maze.

XXVII

But see, the Virgin blest
Hath laid her Babe to rest;
   Time is our tedious song should here have ending;
Heaven's youngest-teemèd star   240
Hath fixed her polished car,
   Her sleeping Lord with handmaid lamp attending;
And all about the courtly stable
Bright-harnessed angels sit in order serviceable.

L'ALLEGRO

Hence, loathèd Melancholy,
  Of Cerberus and blackest Midnight born
In Stygian cave forlorn,
   'Mongst horrid shapes and shrieks and sights unholy!
Find out some uncouth cell   5
  Where brooding Darkness spreads his jealous wings
And the night-raven sings;
  There under ebon shades and low-browed rocks,
As ragged as thy locks,
  In dark Cimmerian desert ever dwell.   10

  But come, thou Goddess fair and free,
In Heaven yclept Euphrosyne,
And by men heart-easing Mirth,
Whom lovely Venus at a birth
With two sister Graces more   15
To ivy-crownèd Bacchus bore;
Or whether (as some sager sing)
The frolic wind that breathes the spring,
Zephyr, with Aurora playing,
As he met her once a-Maying,   20
There on beds of violets blue
And fresh-blown roses washed in dew
Filled her with thee, a daughter fair,
So buxom, blithe, and debonair.
  Haste thee, Nymph, and bring with thee   25
Jest and youthful Jollity,
Quips and cranks and wanton wiles

Nods and becks and wreathèd smiles,
Such as hang on Hebe's cheek,
And love to live in dimple sleek;   30
Sport that wrinkled Care derides,
And laughter holding both his sides.
Come, and trip it as you go,
On the light fantastic toe;
And in thy right hand lead with thee   35
The mountain nymph, sweet Liberty;
And if I give thee honour due,
Mirth, admit me of thy crew,
To live with her and live with thee,
In unreprovèd pleasures free;   40
To hear the lark begin his flight
And singing startle the dull night
From his watch-tower in the skies,
Till the dappled dawn doth rise;
Then to come in spite of sorrow   45
And at my window bid good-morrow,
Through the sweet-briar or the vine
Or the twisted eglantine;
While the cock with lively din
Scatters the rear of darkness thin,   50
And to the stack or the barn-door
Stoutly struts his dames before;
Oft listening how the hounds and horn
Cheerly rouse the slumbering Morn,
From the side of some hoar hill   55
Through the high wood echoing shrill:
Sometime walking not unseen
By hedgerow elms, on hillocks green,
Right against the eastern gate
Where the great Sun begins his state   60
Robed in flames and amber light,

The clouds in thousand liveries dight;
While the ploughman near at hand
Whistles o'er the furrowed land,
And the milkmaid singeth blithe,   65
And the mower whets his scythe,
And every shepherd tells his tale
Under the hawthorn in the dale.
    Straight mine eye hath caught new pleasures
Whilst the lantskip round it measures: 70
Russet lawns and fallows gray
Where the nibbling flocks do stray;
Mountains on whose barren breast
The labouring clouds do often rest;
Meadows trim with daisies pied,   75
Shallow brooks, and rivers wide;
Towers and battlements it sees
Bosomed high in tufted trees,
Where perhaps some beauty lies,
The cynosure of neighbouring eyes.   80
Hard by, a cottage chimney smokes
From betwixt two aged oaks,
Where Corydon and Thyrsis met
Are at their savoury dinner set
Of herbs and other country messes,   85
Which the neat-handed Phillis dresses;
And then in haste her bower she leaves
With Thestylis to bind the sheaves,
Or if the earlier season lead
To the tanned haycock in the mead.   90
    Sometimes with secure delight
The upland hamlets will invite,
When the merry bells ring round
And the jocund rebecks sound
To many a youth and many a maid   95

Dancing in the chequered shade,
And young and old come forth to play
On a sunshine holiday,
Till the livelong daylight fail:
Then to the spicy nut-brown ale,   100
With stories told of many a feat,
How fairy Mab the junkets eat;
She was pinched and pulled, she said,
And by the Friar's lantern led;
Tells how the drudging goblin sweat   105
To earn his cream-bowl duly set,
When in one night, ere glimpse of morn,
His shadowy flail hath threshed the corn
That ten day-labourers could not end;
Then lies him down the lubber fend,   110
And stretched out all the chimney's length
Basks at the fire his hairy strength,
And crop-full out of doors he flings
Ere the first cock his matin rings.
Thus done the tales, to bed they creep,   115
By whispering winds soon lulled asleep.
    Towered cities please us then,
And the busy hum of men,
Where throngs of knights and barons bold
In weeds of peace high triumphs hold,   120
With store of ladies, whose bright eyes
Rain influence, and judge the prize
Of wit or arms, while both contend
To win her grace whom all commend.
There let Hymen oft appear   125
In saffron robe, with taper clear,
And pomp and feast and revelry,
With mask and antique pageantry;
Such sights as youthful poets dream

On summer eves by haunted stream.   130
Then to the well-trod stage anon,
If Johnson's learnèd sock be on,
Or sweetest Shakespeare, Fancy's child,
Warble his native wood-notes wild.

   And ever against eating cares   135
Lap me in soft Lydian airs
Married to immortal verse,
Such as the meeting soul may pierce
In notes with many a winding bout
Of linkèd sweetness long drawn out   140
With wanton heed and giddy cunning,
The melting voice through mazes running,
Untwisting all the chains that tie
The hidden soul of harmony;
That Orpheus' self may heave his head   145
From golden slumber on a bed
Of heaped Elysian flowers, and hear
Such strains as would have won the ear
Of Pluto to have quite set free
His half-regained Eurydice.   150

   These delights if thou canst give,
Mirth, with thee I mean to live.

IL PENSEROSO

Hence, vain deluding Joys,
  The brood of Folly without father bred!
How little you bestead,
  Or fill the fixèd mind with all your toys!
Dwell in some idle brain,   5
  And fancies fond with gaudy shapes possess,
As thick and numberless
  As the gay motes that people the sunbeams,
Or likest hovering dreams,
  The fickle pensioners of Morpheus' train.   10

  But hail, thou Goddess sage and holy,
Hail, divinest Melancholy!
Whose saintly visage is too bright
To hit the sense of human sight,
And therefore to our weaker view   15
O'erlaid with black, staid Wisdom's hue;
Black, but such as in esteem
Prince Memnon's sister might beseem,
Or that starred Ethiop queen that strove
To set her beauty's praise above   20
The sea nymphs, and their powers offended.
Yet thou art higher far descended:
Thee bright-haired Vesta long of yore
To solitary Saturn bore;
His daughter she (in Saturn's reign   25
Such mixture was not held a stain).
Oft in glimmering bowers and glades

E   65

He met her, and in secret shades
Of woody Ida's inmost grove,
While yet there was no fear of Jove.   30
   Come, pensive Nun, devout and pure,
Sober, steadfast, and demure,
All in a robe of darkest grain
Flowing with majestic train,
And sable stole of cipres lawn   35
Over thy decent shoulders drawn.
Come, but keep thy wonted state,
With even step and musing gait
And looks commercing with the skies,
Thy rapt soul sitting in thine eyes: 40
There held in holy passion still,
Forget thyself to marble, till
With a sad leaden downward cast
Thou fix them on the earth as fast.
And join with thee calm Peace and Quiet,   45
Spare Fast, that oft with gods doth diet,
And hears the Muses in a ring
Aye round about Jove's altar sing.
And add to these retirèd Leisure,
That in trim gardens takes his pleasure;   50
But first and chiefest with thee bring
Him that yon soars on golden wing,
Guiding the fiery-wheelèd throne,
The Cherub Contemplation;
And the mute Silence hist along,   55
'Less Philomel will deign a song,
In her sweetest, saddest plight,
Smoothing the rugged brow of Night,
While Cynthia checks her dragon yoke
Gently o'er the accustomed oak.   60
   Sweet bird that shunn'st the noise of folly,

Most musical, most melancholy!
Thee, chauntress, oft the woods among
I woo, to hear thy even-song;
And missing thee I walk unseen   65
On the dry smooth-shaven green,
To behold the wandering moon
Riding near her highest noon,
Like one that had been led astray
Through the heaven's wide pathless way,   70
And oft, as if her head she bowed,
Stooping through a fleecy cloud.

    Oft on a plat of rising ground
I hear the far-off curfew sound,
Over some wide-watered shore   75
Swinging slow with sullen roar;
Or if the air will not permit,
Some still removèd place will fit,
Where glowing embers through the room
Teach light to counterfeit a gloom,   80
Far from all resort of mirth
Save the cricket on the hearth,
Or the bellman's drowsy charm
To bless the doors from nightly harm.

    Or let my lamp at midnight hour   85
Be seen in some high lonely tower,
Where I may oft outwatch the Bear,
With thrice-great Hermes, or unsphere
The spirit of Plato to unfold
What worlds or what vast regions hold   90
The immortal mind that hath forsook
Her mansion in this fleshly nook;
And of those demons that are found
In fire, air, flood, or under ground,
Whose power hath a true consent   95

With planet or with element.
Sometime let gorgeous Tragedy
In sceptred pall come sweeping by,
Presenting Thebes, or Pelops' line,
Or the tale of Troy divine,   100
Or what (though rare) of later age
Ennobled hath the buskined stage.
     But O, sad virgin, that thy power
Might raise Musæus from his bower,
Or bid the soul of Orpheus sing   105
Such notes as, warbled to the string,
Drew iron tears down Pluto's cheek,
And made Hell grant what love did seek!
Or call up him that left half-told
The story of Cambuscan bold,   110
Of Camball and of Algarsife,
And who had Canace to wife,
That owned the virtuous ring and glass,
And of the wondrous horse of brass
On which the Tartar King did ride;   115
And if aught else great bards beside
In sage and solemn tunes have sung,
Of turneys, and of trophies hung,
Of forests, and enchantments drear,
Where more is meant than meets the ear.   120
     Thus, Night, oft see me in thy pale career,
Till civil-suited Morn appear,
Not tricked and frounced as she was wont
With the Attic boy to hunt,
But kerchiefed in a comely cloud,   125
While rocking winds are piping loud,
Or ushered with a shower still,
When the gust hath blown his fill,
Ending on the rustling leaves

With minute-drops from off the eaves.   130
And when the sun begins to fling
His flaring beams, me, goddess, bring
To archèd walks of twilight groves,
And shadows brown that Sylvan loves
Of pine or monumental oak,   135
Where the rude axe with heavèd stroke
Was never heard the nymphs to daunt
Or fright them from their hallowed haunt.
There in close covert by some brook,
Where no profaner eye may look,   140
Hide me from day's garish eye,
While the bee with honeyed thigh,
That at her flowery work doth sing,
And the waters murmuring,
With such consort as they keep,   145
Entice the dewy-feathered Sleep;
And let some strange mysterious dream
Wave at his wings in airy stream
Of lively portraiture displayed,
Softly on my eyelids laid;   150
And as I wake, sweet music breathe
Above, about, or underneath,
Sent by some spirit to mortals good,
Or the unseen Genius of the wood.
    But let my due feet never fail   155
To walk the studious cloisters pale,
And love the high embowèd roof,
With antic pillars massy proof,
And storied windows richly dight
Casting a dim religious light.   160
There let the pealing organ blow
To the full-voiced quire below,
In service high and anthems clear,

As may with sweetness through mine ear
Dissolve me into ecstasies 165
And bring all Heaven before mine eyes.
   And may at last my weary age
Find out the peaceful hermitage,
The hairy gown and mossy cell,
Where I may sit and rightly spell 170
Of every star that heaven doth shew,
And every herb that sips the dew;
Till old experience do attain
To something like prophetic strain.
   These pleasures, Melancholy, give, 175
And I with thee will choose to live.

ARCADES

Part of an entertainment presented to the Countess Dowager of Derby at Harefield by some Noble Persons of her Family; who appear on the Scene in pastoral habit, moving toward the seat of state, with this song:

1. SONG

LOOK, Nymphs and Shepherds, look!
What sudden blaze of majesty
Is that which we from hence descry,
Too divine to be mistook?
    This, this is she   5
To whom our vows and wishes bend:
Here our solemn search hath end.
Fame, that her high worth to raise
Seemed erst so lavish and profuse,
We may justly now accuse   10
Of detraction from her praise:
    Less than half we find expressed,
    Envy bid conceal the rest.

Mark what radiant state she spreads,
In circle round her shining throne   15
Shooting her beams like silver threads:
This, this is she alone,
    Sitting like a goddess bright
    In the centre of her light.

Might she the wise Latona be,   20
Or the towered Cybele,

Mother of a hundred gods?
Juno dares not give her odds;
  Who had thought this clime had held
  A deity so unparalleled?   25

As they come forward, THE GENIUS OF THE WOOD *appears,
and, turning toward them, speaks.*

  Gen. Stay, gentle Swains, for though in this
        disguise
I see bright honour sparkle through your eyes;
Of famous Arcady ye are, and sprung
Of that renownèd flood, so often sung,
Divine Alpheus, who by secret sluice channel   30
Stole under seas to meet his Arethuse;
And ye, the breathing roses of the wood,
Fair silver-buskined Nymphs, as great and good.
I know this quest of yours and free intent
Was all in honour and devotion meant   35
To the great mistress of yon princely shrine,
Whom with low reverence I adore as mine,
And with all helpful service will comply
To further this night's glad solemnity,
And lead ye where ye may more near behold   40
What shallow-searching Fame hath left untold;
Which I full oft amidst these shades alone
Have sat to wonder at and gaze upon.
For know, by lot from Jove I am the Power
Of this fair wood and live in oaken bower,   45
To nurse the saplings tall and curl the grove
With ringlets quaint and wanton windings wove,
And all my plants I save from nightly ill
Of noisome winds and blasting vapours chill;
And from the boughs brush off the evil dew,   50
And heal the harms of thwarting thunder blue,

Or what the cross dire-looking planet smites,
Or hurtful worm with cankered venom bites.
When evening grey doth rise, I fetch my round
Over the mount and all this hallowed ground,   55
And early, ere the odorous breath of morn
Awakes the slumbering leaves, or tasselled horn
Shakes the high thicket, haste I all about,
Number my ranks, and visit every sprout
With puissant words and murmurs made to bless.   60
But else, in deep of night, when drowsiness
Hath locked up mortal sense, then listen I
To the celestial Sirens' harmony,
That sit upon the nine infolded spheres
And sing to those that hold the vital shears   65
And turn the adamantine spindle round
On which the fate of gods and men is wound.
Such sweet compulsion doth in music lie
To lull the daughters of Necessity,
And keep unsteady Nature to her law   70
And the low world in measured motion draw
After the heavenly tune, which none can hear
Of human mould with gross unpurgèd ear;
And yet such music worthiest were to blaze
The peerless height of her immortal praise   75
Whose lustre leads us, and for her most fit,
If my inferior hand or voice could hit
Inimitable sounds. Yet, as we go,
Whate'er the skill of lesser gods can show
I will assay, her worth to celebrate,   80
And so attend ye toward her glittering state;
Where ye may all that are of noble stem
Approach, and kiss her sacred vesture's hem.

ii. Song

O'er the smooth enamelled green
Where no print of step hath been,   85
    Follow me as I sing
    And touch the warbled string:
Under the shady roof
Of branching elm star-proof
      Follow me.   90
I will bring you where she sits,
Clad in splendour as befits
    Her deity.
Such a rural Queen
All Arcadia hath not seen.   95

iii. Song

Nymphs and Shepherds, dance no more
    By sandy Ladon's lilied banks;
On old Lycæus or Cyllene hoar
    Trip no more in twilight ranks;
Though Erymanth your loss deplore   100
    A better soil shall give ye thanks.
From the stony Mænalus
Bring your flocks and live with us;
Here ye shall have greater grace,
To serve the Lady of this place.   105
Though Syrinx your Pan's mistress were,
Yet Syrinx well might wait on her.
    Such a rural Queen
    All Arcadia hath not seen.

COMUS

A MASQUE: PRESENTED AT LUDLOW CASTLE, 1634.

THE PERSONS:

The ATTENDANT SPIRIT, afterward in the habit of
THYRSIS.
COMUS with his crew.
The LADY.
FIRST BROTHER.
SECOND BROTHER.
SABRINA, the Nymph.

The Chief Persons which presented were:

THE LORD BRACKLEY.
MR. THOMAS EGERTON, his Brother.
THE LADY ALICE EGERTON.

The First Scene discovers a Wild Wood.

The ATTENDANT SPIRIT *descends or enters.*

Spirit. Before the starry threshold of Jove's court
My mansion is, where those immortal shapes
Of bright aerial spirits live insphered
In regions mild of calm and serene air,
Above the smoke and stir of this dim spot   5
Which men call Earth, and with low-thoughted care,
Confined and pestered in this pinfold here,
Strive to keep up a frail and feverish being,
Unmindful of the crown that Virtue gives,

After this mortal change, to her true servants   10
Amongst the enthron'd gods on sainted seats.
Yet some there be that by true steps aspire
To lay their just hands on that golden key
That opes the palace of Eternity:
To such my errand is; and but for such   15
I would not soil these pure ambrosial weeds
With the rank vapours of this sin-worn mould.
    But to my task. Neptune, besides the sway
Of every salt flood and each ebbing stream,
Took in by lot 'twixt high and nether Jove   20
Imperial rule of all the sea-girt isles
That, like to rich and various gems, inlay
The unadornèd bosom of the deep;
Which he, to grace his tributary gods,
By course commits to several government,   25
And gives them leave to wear their sapphire crowns,
And wield their little tridents. But this isle,
The greatest and the best of all the main,
He quarters to his blue-haired deities;
And all this tract that fronts the falling sun   30
A noble peer of mickle trust and power
Has in his charge, with tempered awe to guide
An old and haughty nation, proud in arms:
Where his fair offspring, nursed in princely lore,
Are coming to attend their father's state   35
And new-intrusted sceptre. But their way
Lies through the perplexed paths of this drear wood,
The nodding horror of whose shady brows
Threats the forlorn and wandering passenger;
And here their tender age might suffer peril,   40
But that by quick command from sovran Jove
I was despatched for their defence and guard;
And listen why, for I will tell you now

What never yet was heard in tale or song,
From old or modern bard in hall or bower. 45
    Bacchus, that first from out the purple grape
Crushed the sweet poison of misusèd wine,
After the Tuscan mariners transformed,
Coasting the Tyrrhene shore, as the winds listed,
On Circe's island fell.—Who knows not Circe, 50
The daughter of the Sun, whose charmed cup
Whoever tasted lost his upright shape,
And downward fell into a grovelling swine?—
This nymph, that gazed upon his clustering locks,
With ivy berries wreathed, and his blithe youth, 55
Had by him ere he parted thence a son
Much like his father, but his mother more,
Whom therefore she brought up and Comus named;
Who, ripe and frolic of his full-grown age,
Roving the Celtic and Iberian fields, 60
At last betakes him to this ominous wood,
And in thick shelter of black shades embowered
Excels his mother at her mighty art,
Offering to every weary traveller
His orient liquor in a crystal glass 65
To quench the drouth of Phœbus; which as they taste
(For most do taste through fond intemperate thirst)
Soon as the potion works, their human countenance,
The express resemblance of the gods, is changed
Into some brutish form of wolf or bear, 70
Or ounce or tiger, hog or bearded goat,
All other parts remaining as they were;
And they, so perfect is their misery,
Not once perceive their foul disfigurement
But boast themselves more comely than before, 75
And all their friends and native home forget,
To roll with pleasure in a sensual sty.

Therefore, when any favoured of high Jove
Chances to pass through this adventurous glade,
Swift as the sparkle of a glancing star   80
I shoot from heaven to give him safe convoy,
As now I do. But first I must put off
These my sky-robes spun out of Iris' woof
And take the weeds and likeness of a swain
That to the service of this house belongs,   85
Who with his soft pipe and smooth-dittied song
Well knows to still the wild winds when they roar
And hush the waving woods; nor of less faith,
And in this office of his mountain watch
Likeliest and nearest to the present aid   90
Of this occasion. But I hear the tread
Of hateful steps; I must be viewless now.

COMUS *enters with a charming-rod in one hand, his glass in the
other: with him a rout of monsters, headed like sundry sorts of
wild beasts, but otherwise like men and women, their apparel
glistering; they come in making a riotous and unruly noise,
with torches in their hands.*

  Comus. The star that bids the shepherd fold
Now the top of heaven doth hold;
And the gilded car of day   95
His glowing axle doth allay
In the steep Atlantic stream;
And the slope sun his upward beam
Shoots against the dusky pole,
Pacing toward the other goal   100
Of his chamber in the east.
Meanwhile welcome joy and feast,
Midnight shout and revelry,
Tipsy dance and jollity.
Braid your locks with rosy twine,   105

Dropping odours, dropping wine.
Rigour now is gone to bed;
And Advice with scrupulous head,
Strict Age and sour Severity
With their grave saws in slumber lie.   110
We that are of purer fire
Imitate the starry quire,
Who in their nightly watchful spheres
Lead in swift round the months and years.
The sounds and seas, with all their finny drove,   115
Now to the moon in wavering morrice move;
And on the tawny sands and shelves
Trip the pert fairies and the dapper elves.
By dimpled brook and fountain brim
The wood-nymphs, decked with daisies trim,   120
Their merry wakes and pastimes keep:
What hath night to do with sleep?
Night hath better sweets to prove;
Venus now wakes, and wakens Love.
Come, let us our rites begin;   125
'Tis only daylight that makes sin,
Which these dun shades will ne'er report.
Hail, goddess of nocturnal sport,
Dark-veiled Cotytto, to whom the secret flame
Of midnight torches burns! mysterious dame,   130
That ne'er art called but when the dragon womb
Of Stygian darkness spets her thickest gloom
And makes one blot of all the air.
Stay thy cloudy ebon chair,
Wherein thou rid'st with Hecat', and befriend   135
Us thy vowed priests, till utmost end
Of all thy dues be done and none left out,
Ere the blabbing eastern scout,
The nice Morn on the Indian steep,

From her cabined loophole peep 140
And to the tell-tale Sun descry
Our concealed solemnity.
Come, knit hands and beat the ground
In a light fantastic round.

The Measure

Break off, break off, I feel the different pace 145
Of some chaste footing near about this ground.
Run to your shrouds within these brakes and trees;
Our number may affright. Some virgin sure
(For so I can distinguish by mine art)
Benighted in these woods. Now to my charms, 150
And to my wily trains; I shall ere long
Be well stocked with as fair a herd as grazed
About my mother Circe. Thus I hurl
My dazzling spells into the spongy air,
Of power to cheat the eye with blear illusion 155
And give it false presentments, lest the place
And my quaint habits breed astonishment,
And put the damsel to suspicious flight;
Which must not be, for that's against my course.
I, under fair pretence of friendly ends, 160
And well-placed words of glozing courtesy,
Baited with reasons not unplausible,
Wind me into the easy-hearted man
And hug him into snares. When once her eye
Hath met the virtue of this magic dust, 165
I shall appear some harmless villager
Whom thrift keeps up about his country gear.
But here she comes; I fairly step aside
And hearken if I may her business hear.

The LADY *enters*

Lady. This way the noise was, if mine ears be
  true,   170
My best guide now; methought it was the sound
Of riot and ill-managed merriment,
Such as the jocund flute or gamesome pipe
Stirs up among the loose unlettered hinds,
When, for their teeming flocks and granges full,   175
In wanton dance they praise the bounteous Pan,
And thank the gods amiss. I should be loth
To meet the rudeness and swilled insolence
Of such late wassailers; yet, O, where else
Shall I inform my unacquainted feet   180
In the blind mazes of this tangled wood?
My brothers, when they saw me wearied out
With this long way, resolving here to lodge
Under the spreading favour of these pines,
Stepped, as they said, to the next thicket side   185
To bring me berries or such cooling fruit
As the kind hospitable woods provide.
They left me then when the gray-hooded Even,
Like a sad votarist in palmer's weed,
Rose from the hindmost wheels of Phœbus' wain.   190
But where they are, and why they come not back,
Is now the labour of my thoughts. 'Tis likeliest
They had engaged their wandering steps too far,
And envious darkness, ere they could return,
Had stole them from me: else, O thievish Night,   195
Why shouldst thou, but for some felonious end,
In thy dark lantern thus close up the stars
That Nature hung in heaven, and filled their lamps
With everlasting oil, to give due light
To the misled and lonely traveller?   200

F

This is the place, as well as I may guess,
Whence even now the tumult of loud mirth
Was rife and perfect in my listening ear,
Yet nought but single darkness do I find.
What might this be? A thousand fantasies   205
Begin to throng into my memory,
Of calling shapes, and beckoning shadows dire,
And airy tongues that syllable men's names
On sands and shores and desert wildernesses.
These thoughts may startle well but not astound   210
The virtuous mind, that ever walks attended
By a strong siding champion, Conscience.
O, welcome, pure-eyed Faith, white-handed Hope,
Thou hovering angel girt with golden wings,
And thou unblemished form of Chastity!   215
I see ye visibly, and now believe
That he, the supreme good, to whom all things ill
Are but as slavish officers of vengeance,
Would send a glistering guardian, if need were,
To keep my life and honour unassailed.   220
Was I deceived, or did a sable cloud
Turn forth her silver lining on the night?
I did not err; there does a sable cloud
Turn forth her silver lining on the night,
And casts a gleam over this tufted grove.   225
I cannot hallo to my brothers, but
Such noise as I can make to be heard farthest
I'll venture; for my new-enlivened spirits
Prompt me, and they perhaps are not far off.

SONG

Sweet Echo, sweetest nymph, that liv'st unseen   230
   Within thy airy shell
  By slow Meander's margent green,

And in the violet-embroidered vale
  Where the love-lorn nightingale
Nightly to thee her sad song mourneth well;   235
Canst thou not tell me of a gentle pair
  That likest thy Narcissus are?
    O, if thou have
  Hid them in some flowery cave,
    Tell me but where   240
Sweet Queen of Parley, Daughter of the Sphere.
  So mayst thou be translated to the skies,
And give resounding grace to all Heaven's harmonies.

Enter COMUS

Comus. Can any mortal mixture of earth's mould
Breathe such divine enchanting ravishment?   245
Sure something holy lodges in that breast
And with these raptures moves the vocal air
To testify his hidden residence.
How sweetly did they float upon the wings
Of silence, through the empty-vaulted night,   250
At every fall smoothing the raven down
Of darkness till it smiled! I have oft heard
My mother Circe with the Sirens three,
Amidst the flowery-kirtled Naiades,
Culling their potent herbs and baleful drugs,   255
Who, as they sung, would take the prisoned soul
And lap it in Elysium; Scylla wept
And chid her barking waves into attention,
And fell Charybdis murmured soft applause.
Yet they in pleasing slumber lulled the sense   260
And in sweet madness robbed it of itself;
But such a sacred and home-felt delight,
Such sober certainty of waking bliss,
I never heard till now. I'll speak to her,

And she shall be my queen.—Hail, foreign wonder! 265
Whom certain these rough shades did never breed,
Unless the goddess that in rural shrine
Dwellest here with Pan or Sylvan, by blest song
Forbidding every bleak unkindly fog
To touch the prosperous growth of this tall wood. 270
    Lady. Nay, gentle shepherd, ill is lost that praise
That is addressed to unattending ears.
Not any boast of skill, but extreme shift
How to regain my severed company,
Compelled me to wake the courteous Echo   275
To give me answer from her mossy couch.
    Comus. What chance, good lady, hath bereft you
        thus?
    Lady. Dim darkness and this leavy labyrinth.
    Comus. Could that divide you from near-ushering
        guides?
    Lady. They left me weary on a grassy turf.   280
    Comus. By falsehood, or discourtesy, or why?
    Lady. To seek i' the valley some cool friendly spring.
    Comus. And left your fair side all unguarded, lady?
    Lady. They were but twain and purposed quick return.
    Comus. Perhaps forestalling night prevented
        them.   285
    Lady. How easy my misfortune is to hit!
    Comus. Imports their loss beside the present need?
    Lady. No less than if I should my brothers lose.
    Comus. Were they of manly prime, or youthful
        bloom?
    Lady. As smooth as Hebe's their unrazored lips.   290
    Comus. Two such I saw, what time the laboured ox
In his loose traces from the furrow came,
And the swinked hedger at his supper sat.
I saw them under a green mantling vine

That crawls along the side of yon small hill,   295
Plucking ripe clusters from the tender shoots;
Their port was more than human, as they stood:
I took it for a faery vision
Of some gay creatures of the element,
That in the colours of the rainbow live   300
And play i' the plighted clouds. I was awe-strook
And, as I passed, I worshipped. If those you seek,
It were a journey like the path to Heaven
To help you find them.

    Lady   Gentle villager,
What readiest way would bring me to that place?   305
  Comus. Due west it rises from this shrubby point.
  Lady. To find that out, good shepherd, I suppose,
In such a scant allowance of starlight,
Would over-task the best land-pilot's art
Without the sure guess of well practised feet.   310
  Comus. I know each lane and every alley green,
Dingle or bushy dell of this wild wood,
And every bosky bourn from side to side,
My daily walks and ancient neighbourhood;
And if your stray attendance be yet lodged   315
Or shroud within these limits, I shall know
Ere morrow wake or the low-roosted lark
From her thatched pallet rouse. If otherwise,
I can conduct you, lady, to a low
But loyal cottage, where you may be safe   320
Till further quest.
    Lady.   Shepherd, I take thy word,
And trust thy honest-offered courtesy,
Which oft is sooner found in lowly sheds
With smoky rafters than in tapestry halls
And courts of princes, where it first was named,   325
And yet is most pretended. In a place

Less warranted than this or less secure
I cannot be, that I should fear to change it.—
Eye me, blest Providence, and square my trial
To my proportioned strength!—Shepherd, lead on. 330

Enter the two BROTHERS

First Brother. Unmuffle, ye faint stars, and thou, fair
      moon,
That wont'st to love the traveller's benison,
Stoop thy pale visage through an amber cloud,
And disinherit Chaos, that reigns here
In double night of darkness and of shades: 335
Or if your influence be quite dammed up
With black usurping mists, some gentle taper,
Though a rush candle from the wicker hole
Of some clay habitation, visit us
With thy long levelled rule of streaming light,   340
And thou shalt be our star of Arcady
Or Tyrian Cynosure.
    Second Brother.   Or if our eyes
Be barred that happiness, might we but hear
The folded flocks penned in their wattled cotes,
Or sound of pastoral reed with oaten stops,   345
Or whistle from the lodge, or village cock
Count the night watches to his feathery dames,
'Twould be some solace yet, some little cheering,
In this close dungeon of innumerous boughs.
But O that hapless virgin, our lost sister!   350
Where may she wander now, whither betake her
From the chill dew, amongst rude burs and thistles?
Perhaps some cold bank is her bolster now,
Or 'gainst the rugged bark of some broad elm
Leans her unpillowed head, fraught with sad fears. 355
What if in wild amazement and affright,

Or, while we speak, within the direful grasp
Of savage hunger or of savage heat?
   First Brother. Peace, brother, be not over-exquisite
To cast the fashion of uncertain evils;   360
For grant they be so, while they rest unknown,
What need a man forestall his date of grief,
And run to meet what he would most avoid?
Or if they be but false alarms of fear,
How bitter is such self-delusion!   365
I do not think my sister so to seek,
Or so unprincipled in virtue's book,
And the sweet peace that goodness bosoms ever,
As that the single want of light and noise
(Not being in danger, as I trust she is not)   370
Could stir the constant mood of her calm thoughts,
And put them into misbecoming plight.
Virtue could see to do what Virtue would
By her own radiant light, though sun and moon
Were in the flat sea sunk. And Wisdom's self   375
Oft seeks to sweet retirèd solitude,
Where, with her best nurse Contemplation,
She plumes her feathers and lets grow her wings,
That in the various bustle of resort
Were all to-ruffled and sometimes impaired.   380
He that has light within his own clear breast
May sit i' the centre and enjoy bright day:
But he that hides a dark soul and foul thoughts
Benighted walks under the mid-day sun;
Himself is his own dungeon.
   Second Brother.   'Tis most true   385
That musing Meditation most affects
The pensive secrecy of desert cell,
Far from the cheerful haunt of men and herds,
And sits as safe as in a senate-house;

For who would rob a hermit of his weeds,   390
His few books or his beads or maple dish,
Or do his gray hairs any violence?
But Beauty, like the fair Hesperian tree
Laden with blooming gold, had need the guard
Of dragon watch with unenchanted eye,   395
To save her blossoms and defend her fruit
From the rash hand of bold Incontinence.
You may as well spread out the unsunned heaps
Of miser's treasure by an outlaw's den
And tell me it is safe, as bid me hope   400
Danger will wink on opportunity
And let a single helpless maiden pass
Uninjured in this wild surrounding waste.
Of night or loneliness it recks me not;
I fear the dread events that dog them both   405
Lest some ill-greeting touch attempt the person
Of our unownèd sister.
   First Brother.   I do not, brother,
Infer as if I thought my sister's state
Secure without all doubt or controversy:
Yet where an equal poise of hope and fear   410
Does arbitrate the event, my nature is
That I incline to hope rather than fear
And gladly banish squint suspicion.
My sister is not so defenceless left
As you imagine; she has a hidden strength   415
Which you remember not.
   Second Brother.   What hidden strength,
Unless the strength of Heaven, if you mean that?
   First Brother. I mean that too, but yet a hidden
       strength,
Which, if Heaven gave it, may be termed her own.
'Tis chastity, my brother, chastity: 420

She that has that is clad in complete steel,
And, like a quivered nymph with arrows keen,
May trace huge forests and unharboured heaths,
Infamous hills and sandy perilous wilds,
Where, through the sacred rays of chastity,   425
No savage fierce, bandit, or mountaineer
Will dare to soil her virgin purity.
Yea, there where very desolation dwells,
By grots and caverns shagg'd with horrid shades,
She may pass on with unblenched majesty,   430
Be it not done in pride or in presumption.
Some say no evil thing that walks by night,
In fog or fire, by lake or moorish fen,
Blue meagre hag, or stubborn unlaid ghost
That breaks his magic chains at curfew time,   435
No goblin or swart fairy of the mine,
Hath hurtful power o'er true virginity.
Do ye believe me yet, or shall I call
Antiquity from the old schools of Greece
To testify the arms of chastity?   440
Hence had the huntress Dian her dread bow,
Fair silver-shafted queen for ever chaste.
Wherewith she tamed the brinded lioness
And spotted mountain pard, but set at nought
The frivolous bolt of Cupid; gods and men   445
Feared her stern frown, and she was queen o' the
          woods.
What was that snaky-headed Gorgon shield
That wise Minerva wore, unconquered virgin,
Wherewith she freezed her foes to congealed stone,
But rigid looks of chaste austerity,   450
And noble grace that dashed brute violence
With sudden adoration and blank awe?
So dear to Heaven is saintly chastity

That, when a soul is found sincerely so,
A thousand liveried angels lackey her,   455
Driving far off each thing of sin and guilt,
And in clear dream and solemn vision
Tell her of things that no gross ear can hear;
Till oft converse with heavenly habitants
Begin to cast a beam on the outward shape,   460
The unpolluted temple of the mind,
And turns it by degrees to the soul's essence,
Till all be made immortal: but when lust,
By unchaste looks, loose gestures, and foul talk,
But most by lewd and lavish act of sin,   465
Lets in defilement to the inward parts,
The soul grows clotted by contagion,
Imbodies and imbrutes, till she quite lose
The divine property of her first being.
Such are those thick and gloomy shadows damp   470
Oft seen in charnel vaults and sepulchres,
Lingering and sitting by a new-made grave,
As loth to leave the body that it loved,
And linked itself by carnal sensualty
To a degenerate and degraded state.   475
    Second Brother. How charming is divine philosophy!
Not harsh and crabbed, as dull fools suppose,
But musical as is Apollo's lute,
And a perpetual feast of nectared sweets,
Where no crude surfeit reigns.
    First Brother.   List, list! I hear   480
Some far-off hallo break the silent air.
    Second Brother. Methought so too; what should it be?
    First Brother.   For certain,
Either some one like us night-foundered here,
Or else some neighbour woodman, or at worst
Some roving robber calling to his fellows.   485

Second Brother. Heaven keep my sister! Again, again,
and near!
Best draw, and stand upon our guard.
   First Brother.   I'll hallo:
If he be friendly, he comes well; if not,
Defence is a good cause, and Heaven be for us!

Enter the ATTENDANT SPIRIT, *habited like a shepherd.*

That hallo I should know. What are you? speak.   490
Come not too near; you fall on iron stakes else.
   Spirit. What voice is that? my young lord? speak
again.
   Second Brother. O brother, 'tis my father's shepherd,
sure.
   First Brother. Thyrsis! whose artful strains have oft
delayed
The huddling brook to hear his madrigal   495
And sweetened every musk-rose of the dale.
How cam'st thou here, good swain? Hath any ram
Slipped from the fold, or young kid lost his dam,
Or straggling wether the pent flock forsook?
How could'st thou find this dark sequestered nook?   500
   Spirit. O my loved master's heir and his next joy,
I came not here on such a trivial toy
As a strayed ewe, or to pursue the stealth
Of pilfering wolf; not all the fleecy wealth
That doth enrich these downs is worth a thought   505
To this my errand, and the care it brought.
But O, my virgin lady, where is she?
How chance she is not in your company?
   First Brother. To tell thee sadly, shepherd, without
blame
Or our neglect, we lost her as we came.   510
   Spirit. Ay me unhappy! then my fears are true.

    First Brother. What fears, good Thyrsis? Prithee
        briefly shew.
    Spirit. I'll tell ye; 'tis not vain or fabulous,
Though so esteemed by shallow ignorance,
What the sage poets, taught by the heavenly Muse,   515
Storied of old in high immortal verse
Of dire Chimeras and enchanted isles,
And rifted rocks whose entrance leads to Hell;
For such there be, but unbelief is blind.
    Within the navel of this hideous wood,   520
Immured in cypress shades a sorcerer dwells,
Of Bacchus and of Circe born, great Comus,
Deep skilled in all his mother's witcheries;
And here to every thirsty wanderer
By sly enticement gives his baneful cup,   525
With many murmurs mixed, whose pleasing poison
The visage quite transforms of him that drinks
And the inglorious likeness of a beast
Fixes instead, unmoulding reason's mintage
Charactered in the face. This I have learnt   530
Tending my flocks hard by i' the hilly crofts
That brow this bottom-glade; whence night by night
He and his monstrous rout are heard to howl
Like stabled wolves or tigers at their prey,
Doing abhorrèd rites to Hecate   535
In their obscurèd haunts of inmost bowers.
Yet have they many baits and guileful spells
To inveigle and invite the unwary sense
Of them that pass unweeting by the way.
This evening late, by then the chewing flocks   540
Had ta'en their supper on the savoury herb
Of knot-grass dew-besprent and were in fold,
I sat me down to watch upon a bank
With ivy canopied and interwove

With flaunting honeysuckle, and began,   545
Wrapt in a pleasing fit of melancholy,
To meditate my rural minstrelsy,
Till fancy had her fill; but ere a close
The wonted roar was up amidst the woods
And filled the air with barbarous dissonance;   550
At which I ceased and listened them a while,
Till an unusual stop of sudden silence
Gave respite to the drowsy frighted steeds
That draw the litter of close-curtained Sleep.
At last a soft and solemn breathing sound   555
Rose like a steam of rich distilled perfumes
And stole upon the air, that even Silence
Was took ere she was ware and wished she might
Deny her nature and be never more,
Still to be so displaced. I was all ear   560
And took in strains that might create a soul
Under the ribs of Death; but O, ere long
Too well I did perceive it was the voice
Of my most honoured lady, your dear sister.
Amazed I stood, harrowed with grief and fear;   565
And 'O poor hapless nightingale,' thought I,
'How sweet thou singest, how near the deadly snare!'
Then down the lawns I ran with headlong haste,
Through paths and turnings often trod by day,
Till guided by mine ear I found the place,   570
Where that damned wizard, hid in sly disguise
(For so by certain signs I knew) had met
Already, ere my best speed could prevent,
The aidless innocent lady, his wished prey;
Who gently asked if he had seen such two,   575
Supposing him some neighbour villager.
Longer I durst not stay, but soon I guessed
Ye were the two she meant; with that I sprung

Into swift flight, till I had found you here,
But further know I not.
  Second Brother.   O night and shades, 580
How are ye joined with Hell in triple knot,
Against the unarmed weakness of one virgin,
Alone and helpless! Is this the confidence
You gave me, brother?
  First Brother.   Yes, and keep it still;
Lean on it safely: not a period 585
Shall be unsaid for me. Against the threats
Of malice or of sorcery, or that power
Which erring men call Chance, this I hold firm:
Virtue may be assailed but never hurt,
Surprised by unjust force but not enthralled; 590
Yea, even that which mischief meant most harm
Shall in the happy trial prove most glory:
But evil on itself shall back recoil
And mix no more with goodness, when at last,
Gathered like scum and settled to itself, 595
It shall be in eternal restless change
Self-fed and self-consumèd. If this fail,
The pillared firmament is rottenness,
And earth's base built on stubble. But come, let's on.
Against the opposing will and arm of Heaven 600
May never this just sword be lifted up;
But for that damned magician, let him be girt
With all the grisly legions that troop
Under the sooty flag of Acheron,
Harpies and Hydras, or all the monstrous forms 605
'Twixt Africa and Ind, I'll find him out,
And force him to return his purchase back,
Or drag him by the curls to a foul death,
Cursed as his life.
  Spirit.   Alas! good venturous youth,

I love thy courage yet and bold emprise;   610
But here thy sword can do thee little stead:
Far other arms and other weapons must
Be those that quell the might of hellish charm.
He with his bare wand can unthread thy joints
And crumble all thy sinews.

   First Brother.   Why, prithee, shepherd,   615
How durst thou then thyself approach so near
As to make this relation?

   Spirit.   Care and utmost shifts
How to secure the lady from surprisal
Brought to my mind a certain shepherd lad,
Of small regard to see to, yet well skilled   620
In every virtuous plant and healing herb
That spreads her verdant leaf to the morning ray.
He loved me well and oft would beg me sing;
Which when I did, he on the tender grass
Would sit and hearken e'en to ecstasy,   625
And in requital ope his leathern scrip
And show me simples of a thousand names,
Telling their strange and vigorous faculties.
Amongst the rest a small unsightly root,
But of divine effect, he culled me out.   630
The leaf was darkish, and had prickles on it,
But in another country, as he said,
Bore a bright golden flower but not in this soil:
Unknown and like esteemed, and the dull swain
Treads on it daily with his clouted shoon: 635
And yet more med'cinal is it than that moly
That Hermes once to wise Ulysses gave.
He called it hæmony, and gave it me,
And bade me keep it as of sovran use
'Gainst all enchantments, mildew blast, or damp,   640
Or ghastly Furies' apparition.

I pursed it up, but little reckoning made,
Till now that this extremity compelled;
But now I find it true, for by this means
I knew the foul enchanter though disguised,   645
Entered the very lime-twigs of his spells,
And yet came off. If you have this about you
(As I will give you when we go) you may
Boldly assault the necromancer's hall;
Where if he be, with dauntless hardihood   650
And brandished blade rush on him, break his glass,
And shed the luscious liquor on the ground,
But seize his wand. Though he and his cursed crew
Fierce signs of battle make and menace high,
Or, like the sons of Vulcan, vomit smoke,   655
Yet will they soon retire, if he but shrink.
    First Brother. Thyrsis, lead on apace; I'll follow thee,
And some good angel bear a shield before us!

*The Scene changes to a stately Palace, set out with all manner of
    deliciousness; soft music, tables spread with all dainties.
    COMUS appears with his rabble, and the LADY set in an
    enchanted chair; to whom he offers his glass, which she puts
    by and goes about to rise.*

    Comus. Nay, lady, sit; if I but wave this wand,
Your nerves are all chained up in alablaster,   660
And you a statue, or as Daphne was,
Root-bound, that fled Apollo.
    Lady.   Fool, do not boast;
Thou canst not touch the freedom of my mind
With all thy charms, although this corporal rind
Thou hast immanacled, while Heaven sees good.   665
    Comus. Why are you vexed, lady? why do you frown?
Here dwell no frowns nor anger; from these gates
Sorrow flies far. See, here be all the pleasures

That fancy can beget on youthful thoughts,
When the fresh blood grows lively and returns   670
Brisk as the April buds in primrose-season.
And first behold this cordial julep here,
That flames and dances in his crystal bounds,
With spirits of balm and fragrant syrups mixed.
Not that Nepenthes which the wife of Thone   675
In Egypt gave to Jove-born Helena
Is of such power to stir up joy as this,
To life so friendly or so cool to thirst.
Why should you be so cruel to yourself
And to those dainty limbs which Nature lent   680
For gentle usage and soft delicacy?
But you invert the covenants of her trust
And harshly deal, like an ill borrower,
With that which you received on other terms;
Scorning the unexempt condition   685
By which all mortal frailty must subsist,
Refreshment after toil, ease after pain,
That have been tired all day without repast
And timely rest have wanted. But, fair virgin,
This will restore all soon.
   Lady.   'Twill not, false traitor!   690
'Twill not restore the truth and honesty
That thou hast banished from thy tongue with lies.
Was this the cottage and the safe abode
Thou told'st me of? What grim aspects are these,
These ugly-headed monsters? Mercy guard me!   695
Hence with thy brewed enchantments, foul deceiver!
Hast thou betrayed my credulous innocence
With visored falsehood and base forgery?
And wouldst thou seek again to trap me here
With lickerish baits fit to ensnare a brute?   700
Were it a draught for Juno when she banquets,
  G

I would not taste thy treasonous offer. None
But such as are good men can give good things;
And that which is not good is not delicious
To a well-governed and wise appetite.   705
    Comus. O foolishness of men! that lend their ears
To those budge doctors of the Stoic fur,
And fetch their precepts from the Cynic tub,
Praising the lean and sallow Abstinence.
Wherefore did Nature pour her bounties forth   710
With such a full and unwithdrawing hand,
Covering the earth with odours, fruits, and flocks,
Thronging the seas with spawn innumerable,
But all to please and sate the curious taste?
And set to work millions of spinning worms,   715
That in their green shops weave the smooth-haired silk
To deck her sons; and that no corner might
Be vacant of her plenty, in her own loins
She hutched the all-worshipped ore and precious gems
To store her children with. If all the world   720
Should in a pet of temperance feed on pulse,
Drink the clear stream, and nothing wear but frieze,
The All-giver would be unthanked, would be unpraised,
Not half his riches known, and yet despised;
And we should serve him as a grudging master,   725
As a penurious niggard of his wealth,
And live like Nature's bastards, not her sons,
Who would be quite surcharged with her own weight,
And strangled with her waste fertility:
The earth cumbered, and the winged air darked with
       plumes,   730
The herds would over-multitude their lords,
The sea o'erfraught would swell, and the unsought dia-
       monds
Would so emblaze the forehead of the deep

And so bestud with stars, that they below
Would grow inured to light and come at last   735
To gaze upon the sun with shameless brows.
List, lady; be not coy, and be not cozened
With that same vaunted name, Virginity.
Beauty is Nature's coin, must not be hoarded,
But must be current; and the good thereof   740
Consists in mutual and partaken bliss,
Unsavoury in the enjoyment of itself.
If you let slip time, like a neglected rose
It withers on the stalk with languished head.
Beauty is Nature's brag and must be shown   745
In courts, at feasts, and high solemnities,
Where most may wonder at the workmanship.
It is for homely features to keep home;
They had their name thence; coarse complexions
And cheeks of sorry grain will serve to ply   750
The sampler, and to tease the huswife's wool.
What need a vermeil-tinctured lip for that,
Love-darting eyes, or tresses like the morn?
There was another meaning in these gifts:
Think what, and be advised; you are but young yet.   755
   Lady. I had not thought to have unlocked my lips.
In this unhallowed air, but that this juggler
Would think to charm my judgment as mine eyes,
Obtruding false rules pranked in reason's garb.
I hate when Vice can bolt her arguments,   760
And Virtue has no tongue to check her pride.
Impostor, do not charge most innocent Nature,
As if she would her children should be riotous
With her abundance. She, good cateress,
Means her provision only to the good,   765
That live according to her sober laws
And holy dictate of spare Temperance.

If every just man that now pines with want
Had but a moderate and beseeming share
Of that which lewdly-pampered Luxury   770
Now heaps upon some few with vast excess,
Nature's full blessings would be well dispensed
In unsuperfluous even proportion,
And she no whit encumbered with her store:
And then the Giver would be better thanked,   775
His praise due paid; for swinish gluttony
Ne'er looks to Heaven amidst his gorgeous feast,
But with besotted base ingratitude
Crams, and blasphemes his feeder. Shall I go on
Or have I said enough? To him that dares   780
Arm his profane tongue with contemptuous words
Against the sun-clad power of Chastity,
Fain would I something say, yet to what end?
Thou hast not ear nor soul to apprehend
The sublime notion and high mystery   785
That must be uttered to unfold the sage
And serious doctrine of Virginity;
And thou art worthy that thou shouldst not know
More happiness than this thy present lot.
Enjoy your dear wit and gay rhetoric,   790
That hath so well been taught her dazzling fence;
Thou art not fit to hear thyself convinced.
Yet should I try, the uncontrollèd worth
Of this pure cause would kindle my rapt spirits
To such a flame of sacred vehemence   795
That dumb things would be moved to sympathize,
And the brute Earth would lend her nerves and shake,
Till all thy magic structures reared so high
Were shattered into heaps o'er thy false head.
   Comus. She fables not. I feel that I do fear   800
Her words set off by some superior power:

And, though not mortal, yet a cold shuddering dew
Dips me all o'er, as when the wrath of Jove
Speaks thunder and the chains of Erebus
To some of Saturn's crew. I must dissemble,   805
And try her yet more strongly.—Come, no more!
This is mere moral babble, and direct
Against the canon laws of our foundation.
I must not suffer this: yet 'tis but the lees
And settlings of a melancholy blood.   810
But this will cure all straight; one sip of this
Will bathe the drooping spirits in delight
Beyond the bliss of dreams. Be wise, and taste.

The BROTHERS *rush in with swords drawn, wrest his glass out
of his hand, and break it against the ground; his rout make
sign of resistance, but are all driven in. The* ATTENDANT
SPIRIT *comes in.*

   Spirit. What! have you let the false enchanter scape?
O, ye mistook! ye should have snatched his wand,   815
And bound him fast. Without his rod reversed
And backward mutters of dissevering power,
We cannot free the lady that sits here
In stony fetters fixed and motionless.
Yet stay, be not disturbed: now I bethink me,   820
Some other means I have which may be used,
Which once of Meliboeus old I learnt,
The soothest shepherd that e'er piped on plains.
   There is a gentle Nymph not far from hence,
That with moist curb sways the smooth Severn
   stream: 825
Sabrina is her name, a virgin pure;
Whilom she was the daughter of Locrine,
That had the sceptre from his father Brute.
She, guiltless damsel, flying the mad pursuit

Of her enragèd stepdame, Guendolen,   830
Commended her fair innocence to the flood
That stayed her flight with his cross-flowing course.
The water-nymphs that in the bottom played
Held up their pearlèd wrists and took her in,
Bearing her straight to agèd Nereus' hall;   835
Who, piteous of her woes, reared her lank head
And gave her to his daughters to imbathe
In nectared lavers strewed with asphodel,
And through the porch and inlet of each sense
Dropped in ambrosial oils, till she revived   840
And underwent a quick immortal change,
Made Goddess of the river. Still she retains
Her maiden gentleness, and oft at eve
Visits the herds along the twilight meadows,
Helping all urchin blasts and ill-luck signs   845
That the shrewd meddling elf delights to make,
Which she with precious vialed liquors heals;
For which the shepherds at their festivals
Carol her goodness loud in rustic lays
And throw sweet garland wreaths into her stream   850
Of pansies, pinks, and gaudy daffodils.
And, as the old swain said, she can unlock
The clasping charm and thaw the numbing spell,
If she be right invoked in warbled song;
For maidenhood she loves and will be swift   855
To aid a virgin, such as was herself,
In hard-besetting need. This will I try,
And add the power of some adjuring verse.

Song

Sabrina fair,
  Listen where thou art sitting   860
Under the glassy, cool, translucent wave,

In twisted braids of lilies knitting
The loose train of thy amber-dropping hair;
  Listen for dear honour's sake,
  Goddess of the silver lake,   865
    Listen and save!

Listen and appear to us
In the name of great Oceanus;
By the earth-shaking Neptune's mace
And Tethys' grave majestic pace;   870
By hoary Nereus' wrinkled look
And the Carpathian wizard's hook;
By scaly Triton's winding shell
And old soothsaying Glaucus' spell;
By Leucothea's lovely hands   875
And her son that rules the strands;
By Thetis' tinsel-slippered feet
And the songs of Sirens sweet;
By dead Parthenope's dear tomb,
And fair Ligea's golden comb,   880
Wherewith she sits on diamond rocks
Sleeking her soft alluring locks;
By all the nymphs that nightly dance
Upon thy streams with wily glance,
Rise, rise, and heave thy rosy head   885
From thy coral-paven bed,
And bridle in thy headlong wave,
Till thou our summons answered have.
    Listen and save!

SABRINA *rises, attended by water-nymphs, and sings.*

  By the rushy-fringed bank,   890
  Where grow the willow and the osier dank,
    My sliding chariot stays,

Thick set with agate and the azurn sheen
Of turkis blue and emerald green
 That in the channel strays;   895
Whilst from off the waters fleet
Thus I set my printless feet
O'er the cowslip's velvet head,
That bends not as I tread.
Gentle swain, at thy request   900
  I am here!

Spirit. Goddess dear,
We implore thy powerful hand
To undo the charmèd band
Of true virgin here distrest,   905
Through the force and through the wile
Of unblest enchanter vile.
 Sabrina. Shepherd, 'tis my office best
To help ensnarèd chastity.
Brightest lady, look on me.   910
Thus I sprinkle on thy breast
Drops that from my fountain pur :
I have kept of precious cure;
Thrice upon thy finger's tip,
Thrice upon thy rubied lip: 915
Next this marble venomed seat,
Smeared with gums of glutinous heat,
I touch with chaste palms moist and cold.
Now the spell hath lost his hold;
And I must haste ere morning hour   920
To wait in Amphitrite's bower.

SABRINA *descends, and the* LADY *rises out of her seat.*

 Spirit. Virgin daughter of Locrine,
Sprung of old Anchises' line,

May thy brimmèd waves for this
Their full tribute never miss   925
From a thousand petty rills
That tumble down the snowy hills;
Summer drouth or singed air
Never scorch thy tresses fair,
Nor wet October's torrent flood   930
Thy molten crystal fill with mud;
May thy billows roll ashore
The beryl and the golden ore;
May thy lofty head be crowned
With many a tower and terrace round,   935
And here and there thy banks upon
With groves of myrrh and cinnamon.
    Come, lady, while Heaven lends us grace,
Let us fly this cursèd place,
Lest the sorcerer us entice   940
With some other new device.
Not a waste or needless sound
Till we come to holier ground.
I shall be your faithful guide
Through this gloomy covert wide;   945
And not many furlongs thence
Is your father's residence,
Where this night are met in state
Many a friend to gratulate
His wished presence, and beside   950
All the swains that there abide
With jigs and rural dance resort.
We shall catch them at their sport,
And our sudden coming there
Will double all their mirth and cheer.   955
Come, let us haste: the stars grow high,
But Night sits monarch yet in the mid-sky.

*The Scene changes, presenting Ludlow town and the President's
castle; then come in Country Dancers; after them the* ATTEN-
DANT SPIRIT, *with the two* BROTHERS *and the* LADY.

SONG

SPIRIT. *Back, shepherds, back! enough your play*
Till next sunshine holiday.
Here be, without duck or nod, 960
Other trippings to be trod
Of lighter toes, and such court guise
As Mercury did first devise
With the mincing Dryades
On the lawns and on the leas. 965

This second Song presents them to their Father and Mother.

Noble lord and lady bright,
I have brought ye new delight.
Here behold so goodly grown
Three fair branches of your own.
Heaven hath timely tried their youth, 970
Their faith, their patience, and their truth,
And sent them here through hard assays
With a crown of deathless praise,
To triumph in victorious dance
O'er sensual folly and intemperance. 975

The dances ended, the SPIRIT *epiloguizes.*

Spirit. To the ocean now I fly,
And those happy climes that lie
Where day never shuts his eye,
Up in the broad fields of the sky.
There I suck the liquid air 980
All amidst the gardens fair

Of Hesperus and his daughters three
That sing about the golden tree.
Along the crispèd shades and bowers
Revels the spruce and jocund Spring;   985
The Graces and the rosy-bosomed Hours
Thither all their bounties bring.
There eternal summer dwells,
And west winds with musky wing
About the cedarn alleys fling   990
Nard and cassia's balmy smells.
Iris there with humid bow
Waters the odorous banks, that blow
Flowers of more mingled hue
Than her purfled scarf can shew;   995
And drenches with Elysian dew
(List mortals if your ears be true)
Beds of hyacinth and roses,
Where young Adonis oft reposes,
Waxing well of his deep wound   1000
In slumber soft, and on the ground
Sadly sits the Assyrian queen.
But far above in spangled sheen
Celestial Cupid, her famed son, advanced
Holds his dear Psyche sweet entranced   1005
After her wandering labours long,
Till free consent the gods among
Make her his eternal bride,
And from her fair unspotted side
Two blissful twins are to be born,   1010
Youth and Joy; so Jove hath sworn.

    But now my task is smoothly done,
I can fly, or I can run
Quickly to the green earth's end,

Where the bowed welkin slow doth bend,   1015
And from thence can soar as soon
To the corners of the moon.
    Mortals, that would follow me,
Love Virtue; she alone is free.
She can teach ye how to climb   1020
Higher than the sphery chime;
Or, if Virtue feeble were,
Heaven itself would stoop to her.

LYCIDAS

In this Monody the author bewails a learned Friend, unfortunately drowned in his passage from Chester on the Irish seas, 1637; and by occasion foretells the ruin of our corrupted Clergy, then in their height.

YET once more, O ye laurels, and once more,
Ye myrtles brown, with ivy never sere,
I come to pluck your berries harsh and crude,
And with forced fingers rude
Shatter your leaves before the mellowing year.   5
Bitter constraint and sad occasion dear
Compel me to disturb your season due;
For Lycidas is dead, dead ere his prime,
Young Lycidas, and hath not left his peer.
Who would not sing for Lycidas? He knew   10
Himself to sing and build the lofty rhyme.
He must not float upon his watery bier
Unwept, and welter to the parching wind
Without the meed of some melodious tear.
   Begin then, Sisters of the sacred well   15
That from beneath the seat of Jove doth spring,
Begin, and somewhat loudly sweep the string.
Hence with denial vain and coy excuse;
So may some gentle Muse
With lucky words favour my destined urn,   20
And as he passes turn
And bid fair peace be to my sable shroud;
For we were nursed upon the selfsame hill,
Fed the same flock by fountain, shade, and rill;

Together both, ere the high lawns appeared   25
Under the opening eyelids of the morn,
We drove afield, and both together heard
What time the gray-fly winds her sultry horn,
Battening our flocks with the fresh dews of night
Oft till the star that rose at evening bright   30
Toward heaven's descent had sloped his westering wheel.
Meanwhile the rural ditties were not mute,
Tempered to the oaten flute;
Rough Satyrs danced, and Fauns with cloven heel
From the glad sound would not be absent long,   35
And old Damœtas loved to hear our song.

   But O the heavy change, now thou art gone,
Now thou art gone and never must return!
Thee, shepherd, thee the woods and desert caves,
With wild thyme and the gadding vine o'ergrown,   40
And all their echoes mourn.
The willows and the hazel copses green
Shall now no more be seen
Fanning their joyous leaves to thy soft lays.
As killing as the canker to the rose,   45
Or taint-worm to the weanling herds that graze,
Or frost to flowers that their gay wardrope wear,
When first the white-thorn blows,
Such, Lycidas, thy loss to shepherd's ear.

      Where were ye, Nymphs, when the remorseless deep 50
Closed o'er the head of your loved Lycidas?
For neither were ye playing on the steep
Where your old bards, the famous Druids, lie,
Nor on the shaggy top of Mona high,
Nor yet where Deva spreads her wizard stream.   55
Ay me, I fondly dream
"Had ye been there"—for what could that have done?
What could the Muse herself that Orpheus bore,

The Muse herself, for her enchanting son,
Whom universal nature did lament,   60
When by the rout that made the hideous roar
His gory visage down the stream was sent,
Down the swift Hebrus to the Lesbian shore?
      Alas! what boots it with uncessant care
To tend the homely slighted shepherd's trade,   65
And strictly meditate the thankless Muse?
Were it not better done, as others use,
To sport with Amaryllis in the shade
Or with the tangles of Neæra's hair?
Fame is the spur that the clear spirit doth raise   70
(That last infirmity of noble mind)
To scorn delights and live laborious days;
But the fair guerdon when we hope to find
And think to burst out into sudden blaze,
Comes the blind Fury with the abhorred shears,   75
And slits the thin-spun life. "But not the praise,"
Phœbus replied, and touched my trembling ears;
"Fame is no plant that grows on mortal soil,
Nor in the glistering foil
Set off to the world, nor in broad rumour lies,   80
But lives and spreads aloft by those pure eyes
And perfect witness of all-judging Jove;
As he pronounces lastly on each deed,
Of so much fame in Heaven expect thy meed."
      O fountain Arethuse, and thou honoured flood,   85
Smooth-sliding Mincius, crowned with vocal reeds,
That strain I heard was of a higher mood.
But now my oat proceeds,
And listens to the herald of the sea
That came in Neptune's plea.   90
He asked the waves and asked the felon winds,
What hard mishap hath doomed this gentle swain?

And questioned every gust of rugged wings
That blows from off each beakèd promontory.
They knew not of his story;   95
And sage Hippotades their answer brings,
That not a blast was from his dungeon strayed:
The air was calm, and on the level brine
Sleek Panope with all her sisters played.
It was that fatal and perfidious bark,   100
Built in the eclipse and rigged with curses dark,
That sunk so low that sacred head of thine.

   Next Camus, reverend sire, went footing slow,
His mantle hairy and his bonnet sedge,
nwrought with figures dim, and on the edge   105
Like to that sanguine flower inscribed with woe.
"Ah! who hath reft" (quoth he) "my dearest pledge?"
Last came, and last did go,
The Pilot of the Galilean lake;
Two massy keys he bore of metals twain,   110
(The golden opes, the iron shuts amain.)
He shook his mitred locks, and stern bespake:
"How well could I have spared for thee, young swain,
Enow of such as for their bellies' sake
Creep and intrude and climb into the fold!   115
Of other care they little reckoning make
Than how to scramble at the shearers' feast
And shove away the worthy bidden guest.
Blind mouths! that scarce themselves know how to hold
A sheep-hook, or have learnt aught else the least   120
That to the faithful herdman's art belongs!
What recks it them? What need they? They are sped;
And, when they list, their lean and flashy songs
Grate on their scrannel pipes of wretched straw.
The hungry sheep look up and are not fed,   125
But swoln with wind and the rank mist they draw

Rot inwardly, and foul contagion spread;
Besides what the grim wolf with privy paw
Daily devours apace, and nothing said.
But that two-handed engine at the door   130
Stands ready to smite once, and smite no more."
    Return, Alpheus, the dread voice is past
That shrunk thy streams; return, Sicilian Muse,
And call the vales and bid them hither cast
Their bells and flowerets of a thousand hues.   135
Ye valleys low, where the mild whispers use
Of shades and wanton winds and gushing brooks,
On whose fresh lap the swart star sparely looks,
Throw hither all your quaint enamelled eyes,
That on the green turf suck the honied showers,   140
And purple all the ground with vernal flowers.
Bring the rathe primrose that forsaken dies,
The tufted crow-toe and pale jessamine,
The white pink and the pansy freaked with jet,
The glowing violet,   145
The musk-rose and the well-attired woodbine,
With cowslips wan that hang the pensive head
And every flower that sad embroidery wears:
Bid amaranthus all his beauty shed,
And daffadillies fill their cups with tears,   150
To strew the laureate hearse where Lycid lies.
For so to interpose a little ease
Let our frail thoughts dally with false surmise,
Ay me, whilst thee the shores and sounding seas
Wash far away, where'er thy bones are hurled: 155
Whether beyond the stormy Hebrides,
Where thou perhaps under the whelming tide
Visit'st the bottom of the monstrous world;
Or whether thou, to our moist vows denied,
Sleep'st by the fable of Bellerus old,   160
    H

Where the great vision of the guarded mount
Looks toward Namancos and Bayona's hold:
Look homeward Angel now, and melt with ruth,
And, O ye dolphins, waft the hapless youth.

Weep no more, woeful shepherds, weep no more,   165
For Lycidas your sorrow is not dead,
Sunk though he be beneath the watery floor;
So sinks the day-star in the ocean bed,
And yet anon repairs his drooping head,
And tricks his beams, and with new-spangled ore   170
Flames in the forehead of the morning sky:
So Lycidas sunk low, but mounted high,
Through the dear might of Him that walked the waves;
Where other groves and other streams along
With nectar pure his oozy locks he laves,   175
And hears the unexpressive nuptial song
In the blest kingdoms meek of joy and love.
There entertain him all the saints above
In solemn troops and sweet societies,
That sing, and singing in their glory move,   180
And wipe the tears for ever from his eyes.
Now, Lycidas, the shepherds weep no more;
Henceforth thou art the Genius of the shore,
In thy large recompense, and shalt be good
To all that wander in that perilous flood.   185

Thus sang the uncouth swain to the oaks and rills,
While the still Morn went out with sandals gray.
He touched the tender stops of various quills,
With eager thought warbling his Doric lay.
And now the sun had stretched out all the hills,   190
And now was dropped into the western bay.
At last he rose, and twitched his mantle blue:
To-morrow to fresh woods and pastures new.

SONNETS

I

TO THE NIGHTINGALE

O NIGHTINGALE, that on yon bloomy spray
Warblest at eve when all the woods are still,
Thou with fresh hope the lover's heart dost fill
While the jolly Hours lead on propitious May.
'Thy liquid notes that close the eye of day,   5
First heard before the shallow cuckoo's bill,
Portend success in love. O, if Jove's will
Have linked that amorous power to thy soft lay,
Now timely sing, ere the rude bird of hate
Foretell my hopeless doom in some grove nigh;   10
As thou from year to year hast sung too late
For my relief, yet hadst no reason why.
Whether the Muse or Love call thee his mate,
Both them I serve, and of their train am I.

II

ON HIS BEING ARRIVED TO THE AGE OF TWENTY-THREE

How soon hath Time, the subtle thief of youth,
Stolen on his wing my three-and-twentieth year!
My hasting days fly on with full career,
But my late spring no bud or blossom shew'th.
Perhaps my semblance might deceive the truth   5
That I to manhood am arrived so near;
And inward ripeness doth much less appear
That some more timely-happy spirits endu'th.

Yet, be it less or more, or soon or slow,
It shall be still in strictest measure even   10
To that same lot, however mean or high,
Toward which Time leads me, and the will of Heaven.
All is, if I have grace to use it so,
As ever in my great Task-Master's eye.

III

When the Assault was intended to the City

Captain or Colonel or Knight in Arms
Whose chance on these defenceless doors may seize,
If ever deed of honour did thee please,
Guard them, and him within protect from harms.
He can requite thee, for he knows the charms   5
That call fame on such gentle acts as these,
And he can spread thy name o'er lands and seas,
Whatever clime the sun's bright circle warms.
Lift not thy spear against the Muse's bower:
The great Emathian conqueror bid spare   10
The house of Pindarus, when temple and tower
Went to the ground; and the repeated air
Of sad Electra's poet had the power
To save the Athenian walls from ruin bare.

IV

To the Lady Margaret Ley

Daughter to that good Earl, once President
Of England's Council and her Treasury,
Who lived in both unstained with gold or fee,
And left them both, more in himself content,
Till the sad breaking of that Parliament   5
Broke him, as that dishonest victory
At Chæronea, fatal to liberty,

Killed with report that old man eloquent;
Though later born than to have known the days
Wherein your father flourished, yet by you, 10
Madam, methinks I see him living yet:
So well your words his noble virtues praise
That all both judge you to relate them true
And to possess them, honoured Margaret.

V

TO THE LORD GENERAL FAIRFAX AT THE
SIEGE OF COLCHESTER

FAIRFAX, whose name in arms through Europe rings
Filling each mouth with envy or with praise
And all her jealous monarchs with amaze
And rumours loud that daunt remotest kings,
Thy firm unshaken virtue ever brings 5
Victory home, though new rebellions raise
Their Hydra heads and the false North displays
Her broken league to imp their serpent wings.
O yet a nobler task awaits thy hand
(For what can war but endless war still breed?) 10
Till truth and right from violence be freed
And public faith cleared from the shameful brand
Of public fraud: in vain doth Valour bleed,
While Avarice and Rapine share the land.

VI

TO THE LORD GENERAL CROMWELL
ON THE PROPOSALS OF CERTAIN MINISTERS AT THE
COMMITTEE FOR PROPAGATION OF THE GOSPEL

CROMWELL, our chief of men, who through a cloud
Not of war only, but detractions rude,
Guided by faith and matchless fortitude,

To peace and truth thy glorious way hast ploughed,
And on the neck of crownèd Fortune proud   5
Hast reared God's trophies and his work pursued,
While Darwen stream, with blood of Scots imbrued,
And Dunbar field resounds thy praises loud,
And Worcester's laureate wreath: yet much remains
To conquer still; Peace hath her victories   10
No less renowned than War: new foes arise,
Threatening to bind our souls with secular chains.
Help us to save free conscience from the paw
Of hireling wolves whose gospel is their maw.

VII

On his Blindness

When I consider how my light is spent
Ere half my days in this dark world and wide,
And that one talent which is death to hide
Lodged with me useless, though my soul more bent
To serve therewith my Maker, and present   5
My true account, lest He returning chide;
"Doth God exact day-labour, light denied?"
I fondly ask. But Patience, to prevent
That murmur, soon replies, "God doth not need
Either man's work or his own gifts. Who best   10
Bear his mild yoke, they serve him best. His state
Is kingly: thousands at his bidding speed,
And post o'er land and ocean without rest;
They also serve who only stand and wait."

VIII

On the Late Massacre in Piemont

Avenge, O Lord, thy slaughtered saints, whose bones
Lie scattered on the Alpine mountains cold;

Even them who kept thy truth so pure of old,
When all our fathers worshipped stocks and stones,
Forget not: in thy book record their groans   5
Who were thy sheep, and in their ancient fold
Slain by the bloody Piemontese that rolled
Mother with infant down the rocks. Their moans
The vales redoubled to the hills, and they
To heaven. Their martyred blood and ashes sow   10
O'er all the Italian fields, where still doth sway
The triple Tyrant; that from these may grow
A hundredfold, who having learnt thy way
Early may fly the Babylonian woe.

IX

To Mr Lawrence

LAWRENCE, of virtuous father virtuous son,
Now that the fields are dank and ways are mire,
Where shall we sometimes meet, and by the fire
Help waste a sullen day, what may be won
From the hard season gaining? Time will run   5
On smoother, till Favonius re-inspire
The frozen earth and clothe in fresh attire
The lily and rose, that neither sowed nor spun.
What neat repast shall feast us, light and choice,
Of Attic taste, with wine, whence we may rise   10
To hear the lute well touched, or artful voice
Warble immortal notes and Tuscan air?
He who of those delights can judge, and spare
To interpose them oft, is not unwise.

X

To Cyriac Skinner

CYRIAC, whose grandsire on the royal bench
Of British Themis, with no mean applause

Pronounced and in his volumes taught our laws,
Which others at their bar so often wrench,
To-day deep thoughts resolve with me to drench   5
In mirth that after no repenting draws;
Let Euclid rest and Archimedes pause,
And what the Swede intend, and what the French.
To measure life learn thou betimes, and know
Toward solid good what leads the nearest way;   10
For other things mild Heaven a time ordains,
And disapproves that care, though wise in show,
That with superfluous burden loads the day,
And, when God sends a cheerful hour, refrains.

XI

To Cyriac Skinner, on his Blindness

Cyriac, this three years' day these eyes, though clear
To outward view of blemish or of spot,
Bereft of light, their seeing have forgot;
Nor to their idle orbs doth sight appear
Of sun or moon or star, throughout the year,   5
Or man or woman. Yet I argue not
Against Heaven's hand or will nor bate a jot
Of heart or hope, but still bear up and steer
Right onward. What supports me, dost thou ask?
The conscience, friend, to have lost them overplied   10
In Liberty's defence, my noble task,
Of which all Europe talks from side to side.
This thought might lead me through the world's vain
    masque
Content, though blind, had I no better guide.

XII

On his Deceased Wife

METHOUGHT I saw my late espousèd saint
Brought to me like Alcestis from the grave,
Whom Jove's great son to her glad husband gave,
Rescued from death by force though pale and faint.
Mine, as whom washed from spot of child-bed taint   5
Purification in the old Law did save,
And such as yet once more I trust to have
Full sight of her in Heaven without restraint,
Came vested all in white, pure as her mind.
Her face was veiled; yet to my fancied sight   10
Love, sweetness, goodness, in her person shined
So clear as in no face with more delight.
But O, as to embrace me she inclined,
I waked, she fled, and day brought back my night!

NOTES

On the Morning of Christ's Nativity

5. *holy sages:* the Old Testament prophets.

6. *deadly forfeit:* the penalty of death, due to the sin of Adam, which all men inherited, and on account of which God's forgiveness had to be sought.

6. *release,* cancel, remit.

8. *unsufferable,* unbearable, unendurable.

10. *wont,* was wont.

11. *the midst of Trinal Unity.* Together with the Father and the Holy Ghost forming the Holy Trinity.

14. *darksome house of mortal clay:* the body. The poet Denham (contemporary with Milton) said the same kind of thing in the phrase "the soul's dark cottage."

15. *Heavenly Muse.* The Muses were goddesses who inspired men with love of the arts, and whose aid was very often invoked by ancient poets.

19. *the Sun's team.* The Greeks thought that the sun-god (Phœbus Apollo) drove across the sky in a chariot drawn by a team of horses.

20. *Hath took no print of,* is still untouched by.

21. *spangled host:* the stars scattered ('spangled') over the sky, or possibly 'shining'; cf. *Lycidas* (170).

23. *star-led wizards:* the 'Wise Men' of the East, who followed the star to Bethlehem; not 'magicians.'

24. *prevent,* in its original meaning of 'go [or 'arrive'] before.' Notice the fresh but ingenious idea of the Muse hurrying to get there before the Wise Men.

27. *angel quire:* the heavenly host seen by the shepherds.

27. *quire.* The usual spelling of 'choir' in Milton's day.

28. *secret* here probably means 'set apart,' as Milton speaks of "the secret top of Oreb," *Paradise Lost* (I, 6).

122

28. *touched with hallowed fire*, as Isaiah (vi, 6) was inspired when a seraph touched his lips with a live coal from the altar. When speaking of his hopes of writing a great poem some day (in *Reason of Church Government*) Milton says that this needs the help of "that eternal Spirit who can enrich, with all utterance and knowledge, and sends out his Seraphim with the hallowed fire of the Altar to touch and purify the lips of whom he pleases."

30. *While*, when.

33. *doffed*, do off—*i.e.*, put aside. Do off = doff, do on = don; and in Dorset dialect you 'dout' the lamp—do out, put out.

33. *gaudy trim*, gay dress.

36. *her lusty paramour*. Roman poets speak of the sun as the lover of the earth.

39. *guilty front*. Guilty because the whole of nature shared in Adam's sin.

40. *naked*. Like Adam and Eve after the Fall, when they realized that they were naked, and hid themselves from God in shame. Genesis (iii, 7).

41. *Pollute*, polluted.

41. *blame*, fault, crime.

44. *deformities*, ugliness. From the Latin *deformis*, meaning 'ugly,' not 'deformed.'

45. *cease*, stop ('make to cease').

48. *turning sphere*. See Appendix. 'Sphere' here means the whole series of spheres encircling the earth, which made a complete circuit in the twenty-four hours.

50. *turtle wing*: the wings of a turtle-dove—"the dove of peace."

50. *amorous*, crowding round Peace in devotion.

52. *universal peace*. According to the ancient prophecies, the Messiah was to be born at a time of universal peace. There was in fact about the time of the birth of Christ seven years' peace throughout the Roman empire, which included almost the whole known world.

56. *hookèd*, armed with hooks. In the apocryphal II Maccabees (xiii, 2), which Milton would certainly have known, there

is a mention of "chariots armed with hooks"; and Spenser tells of the Sultan's chariot "with iron wheels and hooks armed dreadfully."

59. *awful,* full of awe—*cf.* 'respectful.'

64. *whist,* hushed. So in Ariel's song in *The Tempest* (I, ii, 378), "the wild waves whist."

66. *ocean.* Rhymes with "began," and has three syllables as was usual in Milton's time. So in *The Merchant of Venice* (I, i, 8), "Your mind is tossing on the ocean."

68. *birds of calm.* There was a Greek story that birds called halcyons built nests on the sea in winter (about Christmas-time), and that the sea was always calm till the young birds were hatched.

68. *charmèd,* spell-bound ('under a charm').

69. *amaze,* amazement.

71. *precious influence.* The astrologers thought that the stars shed a sort of invisible liquid ('influence' originally meant something which 'flowed') upon the earth and its inhabitants which affected their lives and destinies. This the stars did by the direction of their beams, sometimes regarded as looking downward. Here all the stars unite in sending a good 'influence' by gazing in the same direction.

74. *Lucifer:* the morning star.

75. *orbs:* spheres. So in Shakespeare's *A Midsummer Night's Dream* (III, ii, 61), we read of "Venus in her glimmering sphere." The spheres were supposed to be transparent (not necessarily invisible), but this would not prevent their shining.

76. *bespake,* spoke. A more emphatic form.

76. *bid,* bade.

78. *given day her room,* made way for day.

79. *The sun himself.* Here is another rather whimsical idea (a little like that of the Muse hurrying to Bethlehem, in l. 24). Milton suggests that the late rising of the sun in winter was caused by its own unwillingness to rise.

81. *as,* as if.

83. *a greater Sun.* Very likely Milton means us to think of "son" as well as "sun." Puns of this sort were liked in his

day, and taken seriously as having a particular meaning. Christ is also "the sun of righteousness," and "the light of men."

83–84. *appear . . . bear.* Probably "appear" was pronounced to rhyme with "bear," which was sometimes spelt 'bare.'

84. *axletree:* the axle of the sun's chariot.

85. *lawn:* grassland or pasture, especially in a clearing in a wood.

86. *Or ere,* before.

87. *simply,* in a simple or homely way.

88. *than,* then. Either spelling could be used in Milton's day.

89. *Pan:* the god of flocks and herds, but also regarded as the god of nature in general. Christ, as the Good Shepherd, was often called Pan at this period, especially in pastoral poetry. See note on l. 183 for the story of the cry "Great Pan is dead," which was later explained as referring to the Crucifixion.

90. *kindly.* Perhaps we have here another instance of double meaning—'kindly' in our sense of the word, and also connected with 'kind,' meaning 'kin,' here suggesting, 'as one of ourselves.'

92. *silly,* homely, simple.

93–148. Read and compare *Arcades* (63–73) with this passage. There are many similarities and also differences. The greatest difference is that here the music is made by the angels, in *Arcades* by the Sirens who guide each sphere. The Fates ("daughters of Necessity") are not mentioned here. But in both passages the nine spheres are mentioned, and both contain the idea that their music controls the world. In *Arcades* Milton says that unregenerate man cannot hear the music; in the Hymn he says that when man does come to hear it he will be purged of sin. You may find more points of agreement and difference if you compare the two passages carefully.

93. The missing of a syllable at the beginning of this stanza gives an idea of the suddenness of the burst of music.

95. *strook,* struck.

97. *noise*. Used of pleasant as well as unpleasant sounds. So in Milton's *At a Solemn Music* the music of the angels is called "that melodious noise." 'Noise' can also mean an actual band or orchestra. *Cf.* Shakespeare, *2 Henry IV* (II, iv, 11), "See if thou canst find out Sneak's noise, Mistress Tearsheet would fain hear some music."

98. *as*, so that it.

98. *took*, captured.

100. *close*, cadence, or end of a musical phrase.

101. *Nature*. Up to this time Nature had held the world together by means of the harmony of the spheres. She now realized that the music made by the angels would be more powerful than hers, and would bind heaven and earth in a more happy bond than her music ever could.

102–103. *hollow round Of Cynthia's seat:* the lowest sphere, namely that of the moon.

103. *Cynthia:* the moon. Artemis, the goddess of the moon, was born on Mount Cynthus in Delos.

103. *airy region.* The 'region of the air' extended above the earth as far as the moon.

103. *thrilling*, piercing. The meaning is, "Nature, which heard such music piercing the region of the air below the sphere of the moon . . ."

112–113. *Cherubim . . . Seraphim.* Plural forms. Medieval theories held that there were nine orders of angels, the Seraphim and Cherubim being the highest.

116. *unexpressive*, inexpressible. *Cf.* Shakespeare, *As You Like It* (III, ii, 10), "The fair, the chaste, and unexpressive she," and Milton, *Lycidas* (176), "the unexpressive nuptial song."

119. *Sons of Morning.* *Cf.* Job (xxxviii, 7), "When the morning stars sang together, and all the sons of God shouted for joy."

122. *the well-balanced world on hinges hung.* *Cf.* Job (xxvi, 7), "He . . . hangeth the earth upon nothing," and *Paradise Lost* (VII, 242), "And Earth self-balanced on her centre hung."

122. *hinges:* the poles.

124. *weltering*, rolling.

125 ff. See Appendix.

132. *consort* means orchestra, also harmony.

135. *Age of Gold*. This is often referred to in Greek and Roman literature. It was believed to be the first period in the history of mankind, when the earth provided freely everything that man required, and he needed to do no work, and lived in perpetual peace and happiness.

136. *speckled*, spotted, defiled. *Cf.* Shakespeare, *A Midsummer Night's Dream* (I, i, 110), "this spotted and inconstant man."

138. *mould*, form, body. "Mould" means both 'shape' and 'earth' (the material of the body). Cf. *Arcades* (72), "which none can hear Of human mould with gross unpurged ear."

141. *Truth and Justice*. Several ideas and legends are joined in these names. According to the Greek story, Justice (who is also called The Maiden and Astræa) lived among men as a kind of guardian spirit, giving all things and maintaining peace. In the Silver Age which followed, when mankind had grown more evil, she retired to the high mountains, but still sometimes visited mankind, to warn them of the consequences if they did not repent. As they grew worse, and the Bronze and Iron Ages followed, she left the earth altogether and became the constellation Virgo (The Maiden) in the heavens. But later the idea grew up that at last the Golden Age would return, and Justice would again dwell on earth. This idea is expressed by Virgil in the Messianic Eclogue (*Eclogue IV*). It was taken up by the early Christians, who interpreted 'the Maiden' of Virgil as the Virgin Mary. The legend of Astræa is also linked with that of the four daughters of God, which arose from the words of *Psalm* 85: "Mercy and Truth are met together: righteousness and peace have kissed each other. Truth shall spring out of the earth; and righteousness shall look down from heaven."

This linking of Greek and Christian beliefs is frequent in Milton.

143. *orbed*, encircled.

143. *like glories wearing*, as gloriously arrayed. Milton originally wrote:

Th' enamelled arras of the rainbow wearing,
And Mercy set between.

146. *tissued.* 'Tissue' meant a fine material with rich colouring,
and usually interwoven with gold or silver thread—not
simply 'thin stuff,' as now. The word gives a good picture of
clouds at sunset or sunrise.

149. *Fate.* In Greek belief, Fate was a power apart from and
stronger than the gods themselves, and controlled the destiny
of men and gods alike. Milton adapts this pagan idea to
Christian thought.

153. *loss,* ruin. Cf. *Paradise Lost* (III, 307–308): Christ "quitted
all to save A world from utter loss."

155. *ychained.* The 'y' is a survival of the old English 'ge'
prefixed to the past participle. It had ceased to be used long
before Milton's day, except in verse, where it gave an idea of
antiquity.

155. *sleep:* of death.

156. *wakeful,* rousing, awakening.

157–160. See Exodus (xix) for the account of Moses receiving
the Ten Commandments. Milton had the idea that the same
trumpet "heard in Oreb" (on Mount Sinai) was "perhaps
once more To sound at general doom." *Paradise Lost* (XI,
74–76).

163. *session.* Three syllables.

164. *in middle air.* Cf. I Thessalonians (iv, 17), "Then we
which are alive and remain shall be caught up together with
them in the clouds, to meet the Lord in the air."

166. *is.* The present tense for the future, to make the picture
more vivid.

168. *The old Dragon.* "And the great dragon was cast out,
that old serpent, called the Devil, and Satan, which deceiveth
the whole world: he was cast out into the earth." (Revelation
xii, 9. *Cf.* xx, 2.)

172. *Swinges,* sometimes spelt 'swindge,' means (i) to beat or
whip, (ii) to move like a lash or whip, as here.

172. *horror.* To say "horror of his tail" instead of "his
horrible tail" gives a more surprising effect.

Stanzas XIX–XXV. Pre-Christian religions overcome by Christ:

> XIX–XX. Greek.
> XXI. Roman.
> XXII–XXV. Syrian and Egyptian.

173. *oracles.* These were an important and practical part of ancient religion, since their advice was believed and acted upon by states as well as by individuals. The most famous oracle was that of Apollo at Delphi, where a priestess who breathed the vapour coming from a chasm in the earth became 'inspired' and spoke for the god. There were many other oracles, often working through dreams.

It was an old tradition that the oracles ceased at the birth of Christ, when all the pagan gods were defeated. Plutarch, who lived at about the time of Christ, wrote an essay, "On the Cessation of the Oracles," in which he offered various explanations, naturally not that given later by Christians— that it was due to the victory of Christ.

174. *voice,* the technical expression among the ancients for the reply given by an oracle.

174. *hum:* the confused speech of the prophetess.

175. *deceiving.* The oracles naturally tried to 'play for safety,' and to avoid committing themselves often gave answers which could bear two meanings. The most famous instance of this was when Crœsus, King of Lydia, asked the Delphic oracle what would happen if he attacked the Greeks; the oracle replied that he would destroy a great empire (which, contrary to his expectations, proved to be his own).

178. *Delphos.* Often used for 'Delphi' in Milton's time.

179. *nightly trance:* dreams at night, in which the god's reply was received.

179. *breathèd spell:* incantation spoken in a whisper.

180. *pale-eyed,* because exhausted by his ecstasy.

180. *cell:* the inner part of the temple, which only the priest might enter.

183. *A voice of weeping heard.* Plutarch, in the essay mentioned

I

above (note on l. 173), tells how the pilot of a ship, when sailing past the island of Paxi, heard a loud voice saying: "When you reach the Palodes, tell them that Great Pan is dead." He did so, and at once "a great groaning was heard, proceeding not from one but from many, mingled with cries of wonder."

185. *poplar pale:* the white poplar.

186. *parting,* departing. Cf. *Paradise Lost* (VIII, 630), "the parting sun."

186. *Genius:* the spirit which guards each place and person.

188. *Nymphs:* semi-divine spirits of nature in the form of maidens.

189. *consecrated earth:* not, as now, a churchyard, but a place consecrated as the home of a god or spirit.

190. *the holy hearth.* The hearth was the centre of the household worship and ritual, a very important part of Roman religion.

191. *Lars.* The *lares* were the spirits presiding over the household.

191. *Lemures:* spirits of the dead, particularly ancestors of the family. Milton gives English forms to both these words, *lemures* having two syllables instead of three as it has in Latin.

192. *urns,* containing the ashes of the dead.

194. *flamens,* priests.

194. *quaint,* elaborate, its usual meaning in Milton's time.

195. *seems to sweat.* Legends of temple statues sweating or bleeding as portents or in times of disaster are related by several ancient writers. Virgil, *Georgics* (I, 480), speaks of the statues in the temples weeping and sweating, among the prodigies which followed the death of Julius Cæsar.

196. *peculiar power:* spirit or god inhabiting a particular place. So the local gods deserted Troy when it was about to fall, Virgil, *Æneid* (II, 352), like rats leaving a sinking ship.

197. The rhythm changes at the first line of Stanza XXII, with the accent on the first syllable. So also in ll. 212, 213, 215, and 218. This gives a feeling of harshness and horror, suited to the crude and cruel religions of which these stanzas speak. The descriptions of the Greek and Roman divinities,

on the contrary, give a feeling of more gentleness and pathos (we feel rather sorry for them) which is helped by the smoother run of the verse.

Compare this passage with the long list of pagan gods (once angels, now fallen) who rallied at Satan's call (*Paradise Lost* I, 392 *ff.*).

197. *Peor and Baalim.* Baalim is the plural form of Baal. Baal was the chief god of the Phœnicians and Canaanites-worshipped under several forms in different places—hence the plural here—one of which was Baal-Peor, from the mountain Peor. The Israelites incurred the anger of God by turning to the worship of Baal-Peor (Numbers xxv, 3).

199. *that twice-battered god:* Dagon. When the Philistines captured the Ark they set it up in the temple of Dagon. But the statue of Dagon fell down before the Ark, and when set up again fell a second time, its head and hands being broken off (1 Samuel v, 4).

200. *Ashtaroth:* the Phœnician Astarte, a moon-goddess ("moonèd"). She was a goddess of fertility ("mother"), and the chief goddess of the Phœnicians. Among her titles were Queen of Heaven and Mother of the Gods.

203. *Lybic Hammon*, or Ammon, was an Egyptian god, represented as a horned ram. (He "shrinks his horn" when overcome by Christ.) His chief shrine was in the desert of Libya.

203. *shrinks.* Active—makes shrink. Cf. *Lycidas* (132–133), "the dread voice is past That shrunk thy streams."

204. *Tyrian:* Phœnician. Tyre was the chief city of Phœnicia.

204. *Thammuz*, the son of a Syrian king, was loved by Ashtoreth (Ashtaroth). He was killed by a boar which he was hunting, but Ashtoreth persuaded the gods of the lower world to allow him to spend half the year on earth with her, the other half being spent in the world below. On earth he lived in a beautiful garden, in the company of Ashtoreth. The Phœnician women held a ceremony of mourning for him every year, a custom which spread to other countries, and was really a lament for the death of the year, a 'vegetation myth.'

The Greeks adopted the legend, transferring it to Adonis

and Aphrodite, the Greek counterparts of Thammuz and Ashtaroth.

205. *Moloch:* a god of the Ammonites, to whom children were cruelly sacrificed. He is often mentioned in the Old Testament.

207. *burning idol.* The statue of Moloch was of brass, and contained a furnace ("the furnace blue").

208. *cymbals' ring.* Used to drown the cries of the victims. Sandys' *Travels,* a book well known in Milton's day, describes the worship of Moloch.

211. *brutish gods of Nile:* the gods of Egypt, often worshipped under the form of animals. Cf. *Paradise Lost* (I, 477)

> A crew who under names of old renown,
> Osiris, Isis, Orus and their train,
> With monstrous shapes and sorceries abused
> Fanatic Egypt and her priests, to seek
> Their wandering gods disguised in brutish forms
> Rather than human.

212. *Isis:* sister and wife of Osiris, represented with the horns of a cow.

212. *Orus* (Horus): son of Isis and Osiris, who had the head of a hawk.

212. *Anubis.* Represented with the head of a dog or jackal.

213. *Osiris:* the chief god of the Egyptians. He was a king of Egypt, who, having civilized his own country, travelled to others to spread civilization. Having returned he was murdered by his brother Set, or Typhon, who cut up his body and scattered the pieces. Isis found them, and Anubis helped to put them together and embalm them. Osiris then came to life again, and reigned as king over the living and judge of the dead.

214. *Memphian grove.* The chief shrine of Osiris was at Memphis. Here there was a sacred bull known as Apis, which was believed to be the incarnation of Osiris and was worshipped as such. The next line, of course, refers to this bull.

215. *unshowered,* because there is little rain in Egypt, the overflowing of the Nile being the chief source of water.

217. *his sacred chest:* the chest in which the body of Osiris was laid.

218. *shroud,* shelter, or cover. Cf. *Comus* (147), "Run to your shrouds within these brakes and trees."

219. *timbrelled anthems dark,* mysterious hymns accompanied on timbrels.

220. *sable-stolèd,* robed in black.

220. *ark.* The statue of Osiris was placed in a small temple of gilded wood.

223. *eyne.* Old form of the plural, used for the sake of the rhyme.

226. *Typhon.* This may be Typhon, brother of Osiris, who was represented in the form of a crocodile. But the Typhon of Greek mythology is more probably meant. He was an ally of the giants who rebelled against Zeus; he was of gigantic size, had a hundred heads, and his body ended in serpent's coils. In sculpture from an old temple in Athens, he has a tail consisting of three serpents twined together—"snaky twine," as here.

228. *in his swaddling bands,* as Hercules strangled the snakes when still in his cradle.

229. *the sun in bed.* Milton here carries the 'conceit' or fancy much further than the slightly comic or fanciful ideas suggested in ll. 24 (the muse running to arrive before the Wise Men) and 79 (the sun wilfully delaying his rising in winter). Here we have a picture of the sun in a 'four-poster' bed with red curtains made of the clouds at sunrise, and just peeping up over a pillow made of a wave as he rises from the sea.

231. *orient,* eastern, as the sun is rising.

This stanza compares Christ putting the old gods to flight with the sun driving away ghosts and fairies at his rising. *Cf.* Shakespeare, *A Midsummer Night's Dream* (III, ii, 380–382):

> yonder shines Aurora's harbinger;
> At whose approach, ghosts, wandering here and there,
> Troop home to churchyards.

232. *shadows pale:* spirits, not the shades of night, which would not be pale.

234. *Each fettered ghost:* spirits of the dead which were still earthbound, unwilling to leave the scene of their earthly life, or unable to rest because of the sins they had committed.

234. *several,* separate, special.

236. *night-steeds,* steeds of night.

236. *moon-loved maze,* paths in the forests in which Diana, the moon-goddess, loved to hunt. Together with Hecate she is goddess of night, and of fairies and ghosts.

240. *youngest-teemèd star.* Latest born. The star seen by the Wise Men which was the newest of the stars.

241. *Hath fixed her polished car.* The star "came and stood over where the young child was." (St Matthew ii, 9.)

243. *courtly,* like a court, because a king was within.

244. *bright-harnessed,* clad in bright armour.

244. *serviceable,* ready to serve.

L'Allegro

Title. 'L'Allegro' means 'the cheerful man.'

1. *Melancholy.* In *L'Allegro* Milton uses the word in what is now its usual sense, of a disagreeable thing. In *Il Penseroso* we shall find the word used in a rather different sense. For the real nature of Melancholy, see note on *Comus* (810).

2. *Cerberus:* the dog with three heads, which guarded the entrance to Hades.

3. *Stygian.* The Styx was one of the rivers which flowed through Hades, and comes to stand for Hades in general. For the adjective 'Stygian' cf. *Comus* (132), "Stygian darkness."

5. *uncouth,* unfamiliar, and so strange, uncanny.

8. *ebon,* black.

8. *low-browed,* frowning, or overhanging.

9. *ragged.* Closely akin to 'rugged'—*cf.* "the ragged rocks" (Isaiah ii, 21).

10. *Cimmerian.* The Cimmerians, according to Homer, lived on the western edge of the world, in a land of perpetual mist and darkness.

11. *fair and free.* These two adjectives are very often used together in descriptions of ladies; it is difficult to say exactly what 'free' means, and very likely it is used more for the sake of the alliteration and sound than with any definite meaning. An eighteenth-century editor says that it "is equal to our phrase of *genteel*, of *free* and easy carriage."

12. *yclept,* called. See note on *Nativity Ode* (155) for the prefix 'y.'

15. *two sister Graces:* Aglaia (festive beauty) and Thalia (the bloom of youth). Euphrosyne means 'mirth.' The three Graces, usually attendant on Venus, were often represented in masques.

17. *as some sager sing*. Both genealogies are Milton's own ideas. Spenser called the Graces the daughters of Jove and Eurynome. Since they were not actual goddesses, the poets were free to invent any pedigree they thought appropriate for them.

18. *breathes*. As we speak of breathing fury, or breathing vengeance.

19. *Zephyr:* the west wind.

24. *buxom* originally meant obedient, then gracious, then lively, as here.

24. *debonair*, courteous, friendly.

These two verse-paragraphs (ll. 1–24) are particularly interesting as an example of the way in which Milton handled verse.

The address to Melancholy has a very melodramatic effect—one can almost hear the voice of the speaker rising at the end of the long line, then dropping to a blood-curdling whisper in the short one. It is clearly a parody.

Then at l. 11 there is a sudden change, with the invocation to Mirth. Ll. 11–18 run along smoothly and easily. Then in ll. 19 and 20 an extra syllable is added, giving a playful effect.

27. *quips:* sharp and witty remarks, repartees. *Cf.* Shakespeare, *As You Like It* (V, iv, 71) (speaking of a courtier's beard), "If I sent him word again it was not well cut, he would send me word he cut it to please himself. This is called the 'quip modest.'"

27. *cranks*. A crank is a twist or turn of any sort, sometimes actually a winding passage. Here it is applied to words, and means a twisted or unexpected use.

27. *wanton wiles*, playful tricks.

28. *becks* is usually taken to mean low bows or curtseys, but if so it comes in rather oddly between nods and smiles. I think it more probably means some movement of the head (an upward nod, for instance) intended to beckon on or invite a person. This meaning seems clear in Burton's lines (*Anatomy of Melancholy*) when he uses "becks," "nods," and "smiles" (very much as in Milton's lines) to translate the one Latin word 'nutus' ("nod").

> With becks and nods he first began
> To try the wenche's mind;
> With becks and nods and smiles again
> An answer he did find.

28. *wreathèd*. We still speak of a person's face as being 'wreathed in smiles'—smiles as it were wreathing or adorning the face, as they "hang" on Hebe's cheek. The meaning is then transferred from the face to the smile itself.

29. *Hebe:* the cup-bearer of the gods, and the personification of Youth.

33. Contrast the invitation to Mirth with that to Melancholy in *Il Penseroso* (31 *ff.*).

34. *fantastic*, sportive. Cf. *Comus* (143–144).

> Come, knit hands and beat the ground
> In a light fantastic round.

36. *The mountain nymph*. It is usual to explain this phrase by saying that Liberty has always been connected with mountains, partly because of their natural wild character, and partly because they have so often been the stronghold of resistance to tyranny. *Cf.* Wordsworth:

> Two Voices are there; one is of the sea,
> One of the mountains; each a mighty Voice:
> In both from age to age thou didst rejoice,
> They were thy chosen music, Liberty!

But one older critic, Warton (eighteenth century), has reason and wit on his side. He says:

Dr Newton supposes, that liberty is here called the mountain nymph, "because the people in mountainous countries have generally preserved their liberties longest, as the Britons formerly in Wales, and the inhabitants in the mountains of Switzerland at this day." Milton's head was not so political on this occasion. Warmed with the poetry of the Greeks, I rather believe that he thought of the Oreads of Greek mythology, whose wild haunts among the romantic mountains of Pisa are so beautifully described in Homer's *Hymn to Pan*. The allusion is general, to inaccessible and uncultivated scenes of nature, such as mountainous situations afford, and which were best adapted to the free and uninterrupted range of the nymph Liberty. He compares Eve to an Oread, certainly without any reference to Wales or the Swiss Cantons, in *Paradise Lost*, IX, 387.

38. *of thy crew*. I.e., to membership of. The word 'crew'
generally has a bad meaning, but has not here; *cf.* its use in
'a ship's crew.'

39. *her*. Liberty's.

40. *unreprovèd*, not to be reproved, blameless. *Cf.* "unenchanted eye," *i.e.*, 'unenchantable' (*Comus* 395). The two
forms were not rigidly distinguished in Milton's day.

42. *dull*, sad, gloomy.

44. *dappled*. A perfect description of the sky at sunrise.

45. *to come*. There has been much discussion about who is to
come—the poet, the lark, Mirth, the dawn. But it is surely
the poet. Two examples of "unreproved pleasures" are
given—"To hear the lark begin his flight," and "To come in
spite of sorrow." (These infinitives are not parallel with
"to live with thee," which depends upon "admit me.") It is
natural to suppose that both actions are performed by the
same person—*i.e.*, the poet—apart from the fact that larks
do not come to windows, nor is it to be expected of Mirth or
of the dawn.

The poet first hears the lark, then rises, and goes to his
window to greet the new day ("bid good-morrow"). The
farmyard is already awake, and soon the sounds of the hunt
are heard. The poet then goes out, to enjoy the sights and
sounds of the countryside. These are among the "unreproved
pleasures" to which he looks forward. Later (69) he finds
yet other pleasures ("new pleasures") of a rather different
kind, but also due to his choice of Mirth.

45. *in spite of sorrow*, in defiance of sorrow.

48. *eglantine* is usually considered to be the same as the sweet
briar, but "twisted" suggests rather honeysuckle. One
need not demand botanical accuracy.

50. *Scatters the rear of darkness thin*, scatters the scanty rearguard
of darkness.

55. *hoar*, grey, as if through age; hence 'antique,' 'ancient.'
For its application to hills *cf.* Spenser, *Fairy Queen* (I, iii, 10),
"Under the steep foot of a mountain hoar."

57. *not unseen*. The 'cheerful man' welcomes publicity, while the
'thoughtful man' shuns it—"I walk unseen," *Il Penseroso* (65).

60. *state*, stately progress. *Cf.* 'to ride in state.' The sun in the heavens was held to correspond to the king on earth. *Cf.* the French phrase, 'le roi soleil.'

62. *liveries:* uniforms of retainers. Though the word can be used of any clothing, the special meaning is appropriate here, the clouds being attendants of the sun. In his *First Prolusion* (see Introduction, p. 18), Milton speaking of the sunrise, says that "the clouds, arrayed in garb of every hue, attend the rising god in festive train and long procession."

67. *tells his tale.* The obvious meaning is "relates his story." a regular pastime of shepherds in all pastoral verse, as they sit "under the hawthorn," or other shady tree. But it has been suggested that the phrase means 'counts his sheep,' as "tale" can mean a count or reckoning. The shepherd counts his sheep as he lets them out of the fold at dawn. This would fit in with the idea that all the activities described in this part of the poem are those of the early morning. I do not, however, think that this is necessarily the case, and it would seem rather forced to put an unusual meaning into such a usual expression as "to tell his tale." And why "under the hawthorn"?

70. *lantskip*, the form of the word always used by Milton. We now say 'landscape.'

71. *lawns.* See note on *Nativity Ode* (85).

71. *russet*, probably a greyish or neutral colour, not reddish-brown. *Cf.* Shakespeare, *Hamlet* (I, i, 166), "the morn in russet mantle clad," and *A Midsummer Night's Dream* (III, ii, 21), "russet-pated choughs," (choughs have grey heads).

75. *pied*, meaning spotted, or parti-coloured, is frequently used to describe flowers; *e.g.*, "daisies pied and violets blue," Shakespeare, *Love's Labour's Lost* (V, ii, 904). To suit this one must take "trim with daisies" together. But the run of the verse would suggest taking "pied" with "meadows" rather than with "daisies," the meaning being 'trim meadows speckled with daisies.'

78. *Bosomed*, hidden.

78. *tufted*, cf. *Comus* (225), "this tufted grove." The meaning probably is 'planted in clumps,' or the word may refer to thick foliage at the tops of the trees.

79. *lies*, dwells. *Cf.* "When the court lay at Windsor." Shakespeare, *Merry Wives of Windsor* (II, ii, 65).

80. *cynosure:* the constellation of the Lesser Bear, which includes the pole-star, by which sailors steered. The word thus comes to mean 'a guiding star,' and so 'an object of special attention.' *Cf. Comus* (341):

> . . . our star of Arcady,
> Or Tyrian Cynosure.

83. *Corydon and Thyrsis.* The names given by Milton to his English shepherds and shepherdesses are those commonly used by Theocritus and other ancient pastoral poets.

85. *messes*, dishes. *Cf.* 'officers' mess.'

91. *secure*, free from care, its original meaning.

94. *rebecks:* a primitive kind of fiddle, only used in country districts after the violin came into use. In Shakespeare, *Romeo and Juliet* (IV, iv, 136), one of the musicians is called Hugh Rebeck.

98. *a sunshine holiday.* *Cf. Comus* (959), "Till next sunshine holiday."

101. *feat . . . eat.* "Eat" is here past tense, probably pronounced 'ate,' "feat" rhyming with it and pronounced 'fate.' *Cf.* note on *Nativity Ode* (83–84).

102. *junkets.* From an Italian word (*giuncata*) meaning food served on reeds, as for example cream cheese; hence any country delicacy. *Cf.* 'junketing,' meaning rustic merrymaking.

103. *pinched and pulled*, the punishment generally inflicted by the fairies, especially for laziness.

104. *And by the Friar's lantern led.* The earlier edition (1645) reads: "And he, by Friar's lantern led," introducing a second speaker. The later edition (1673) probably embodies Milton's own corrections, so it seems best to follow this, in spite of the slight awkwardness of the connexion with: "Tells how the drudging goblin . . ."

104. *Friar's lantern:* the Will-o'-the-wisp, or Jack-o'-lantern, who led travellers astray by night with his deceptive light.

105. *the drudging goblin.* Called Robin Goodfellow, Hobgoblin,

or Puck. Though mischievous, he would work for those who gave him the proper reward of a bowl of milk. In Shakespeare's *A Midsummer Night's Dream* (II, i, 40) the Fairy, speaking to Puck, calls him Robin Goodfellow, and recounts some of his mischievous pranks, adding:

> Those that Hobgoblin call you, and sweet Puck,
> You do their work, and they shall have good luck.

108. *shadowy*, insubstantial, unreal.

110. *lubber*, big and clumsy. So the Fairy calls Puck "thou lob of spirits" in *A Midsummer Night's Dream* (II, i, 16). 'Lob' and 'lubber' are the same word.

110. *fend:* fiend—the old pronunciation, rhyming with 'end.'

111. *chimney:* fireplace.

113. *flings*, dashes.

114. *matin:* the first Church service of the day, to which people were summoned by a bell, as the cock's crowing was the signal for all ghosts, fairies, etc., to depart.

117. *then*, on another occasion. Balancing "sometimes" (91). Here Milton ends his description of country pleasures, and turns to those of the town.

120. *weeds*, garments, as we still speak of 'widow's weeds.'

120. *triumphs*, shows. Bacon wrote an essay "Of Masques and Triumphs."

121. *store of*, plenty of.

122. *rain influence.* See note on *Nativity Ode* (71). Here the ladies' eyes are supposed to be like stars, and to be able to shed an 'influence' as stars do.

119–124. Milton was deeply interested in the old romances and chronicles such as those of Malory, and often refers to them. This interest was shown in his later plan (never carried out) to write an "Arthuriad." Milton wrote of this interest of his:

> That I may tell you whither my younger feet wandered; I betook me among those lofty fables and romances, which recount in solemn cantos the deeds of knighthood founded by our victorious kings; and from hence had in renown over all Christendom.

> *Apology for Smectymnuus*

125. *Hymen:* the god of marriage. He was often represented in masques, dressed in a saffron (yellow) robe and carrying a torch. Here Hymen comes "with taper clear"—*i.e.*, a torch burning brightly; in the *Epitaph on the Marchioness of Winchester* he comes "with a scarce well-lighted flame," because she was to die not long after her marriage.

127. *pomp*, procession.

127. *revelry*. Not vaguely 'fun and games,' but formal theatrical entertainments in great houses, or such as the Master of the Revels arranged for the Court, or the 'Revels' at the Inns of Court.

128. *mask*, or masque, such as Milton's own *Comus*.

128. *pageantry*. Pageants were a kind of 'tableau,' or allegorical group, shown on movable stages, rather like the groups on vehicles in the Lord Mayor's Show.

130. *haunted*. By the water-nymphs. Cf. *Nativity Ode* (184).

131. 'L'Allegro' goes to the theatre in person instead of reading plays as 'Il Penseroso' does.

131. *well-trod*, well-acted.

132. *Jonson*. Ben Jonson was Poet Laureate at this time. He was famous especially for his comedies, which were learned and sometimes rather pedantic.

132. *sock*. Greek and Roman actors wore light slippers called *socci* when the play was a comedy, and 'buskins,' or boots with high heels (which made the actor appear larger than life-size), in tragedies. So 'sock' and 'buskin' came to be used to mean 'comedy' and 'tragedy.' Hence this line means 'if one of Jonson's comedies is being performed.'

133. *Fancy*, imagination, creative faculty. This is the quality of Shakespeare which Milton seems particularly to have admired, and which he singles out for praise in his *Epitaph on Shakespeare*.

134. *native wood-notes wild*. This is often regarded as a somewhat doubtful compliment, and there is in fact some question whether Milton did fully appreciate Shakespeare's genius. But in this place we may remember, first, that Milton is speaking only of the comedies, the tragedies coming into

'Il Penseroso's' sphere; and, secondly, that he is contrasting Shakespeare's natural ("native") ease and grace with Jonson's scholarship and formality.

135. *eating cares*. A phrase translated from Horace. 'Gnawing' is often used in this sense now.

136. *Lydian*. Greek music was composed in one of three 'modes'—the Dorian, the Phrygian, or the Lydian. The difference between them can best be described as resembling the difference between major and minor. The Dorian mode was simple and solemn, the Phrygian warlike, and the Lydian soft and sweet.

139. *bout*, bend or coil—*e.g.*, of a rope or of a snake's tail. Here it is used of a musical phrase which seems to wind along to its close.

141. The figure of speech in which the adjective seems to contradict its noun is known as 'oxymoron.' For another example cf. *At a Vacation Exercise* (52), "willing chains and sweet captivity."

141. *cunning*, art, skill.

142–144. Harmony is represented as bound fast and unable to express itself until released by the singer's voice unfastening its chains by following out the "mazes" (or "winding bouts") of the music.

145. *Orpheus' self*, Orpheus himself.

Orpheus was a legendary poet and musician, who could enchant even the beasts, birds, and trees. On their wedding day his bride, Eurydice, died, and was carried off to Hades. Orpheus followed her, and by his music melted the hearts of the infernal deities and won their permission to take back his bride—but on the condition that he never once looked back at her on the way. This he was unable to carry out, and, as he looked to see if she were following, she was snatched back to Hades.

145. *heave*, lift. *Cf.* "rise, and heave thy rosy head." *Comus* (885).

147. *Elysian*. Elysium was a sort of paradise, to which the souls of some semi-divine or great men were believed to go after death, not as a reward for virtue, but simply because of

their greatness in their own way. Orpheus is in Elysium because he was a great poet.

Milton imagines the music which he hopes to enjoy as being so good that it can reach Orpheus even in Elysium, and as being more moving than even Orpheus' own.

150. *half-regained*, because Eurydice was prevented from following Orpheus all the way back.

151. *if.* A shade of doubt, perhaps which is not present in the ending of *Il Penseroso*.

Il Penseroso

Title. 'Il Penseroso' means 'the thoughtful man.'

3. *bestead*, help, profit.

4. *fixèd*, steady.

4. *toys*, trifles.

6. *fond*, foolish. Cf. *Comus* (67).

6. *possess. I.e.*, endow foolish fancies with gaudy shapes.

10. *pensioners.* Queen Elizabeth had a body-guard of specially chosen noblemen called Pensioners. Hence the word came to be used to mean 'retinue,' or 'attendants.' *Cf.* "The cowslips tall her pensioners be." Shakespeare, *A Midsummer Night's Dream* (II, i, 10).

10. *Morpheus:* the god of sleep (hence our word 'morphia').

12. *Melancholy.* As we shall see, the melancholy of *Il Penseroso* is different from the melancholy of *L'Allegro.* It is not an unpleasant or disagreeable state of mind, and not at all the hateful thing described in *L'Allegro*, but a gentle and mild seriousness or thoughtfulness.

14. *hit*, suit, agree with.

17. *black.* Brunettes were despised in the Elizabethan age, the Queen herself being fair. *Cf.* "Away, you Ethiop!" Shakespeare, *A Midsummer Night's Dream* (III, ii, 257), and "Out, tawny Tartar, out!" (*ibid.*, 263).

17. *esteem:* in the general opinion of men.

18. *Prince Memnon:* a prince of Ethiopia, the handsomest of men, according to Homer (*Odyssey*, XI, 522). His sister Hemera (who is first mentioned in the medieval romances) was equally beautiful.

19. *that starred Ethiop queen:* Cassiopeia, wife of Cepheus king of Ethiopia. According to the usual legend she boasted of the beauty of her daughter Andromeda, claiming that she was more beautiful than the Nereids (sea-nymphs). They, in

anger, persuaded Poseidon to send a flood to inundate Ethiopia, and also a sea-monster. Andromeda was to be offered to this as a victim, but was rescued by Perseus. Cassiopeia was changed into a constellation ("starred"). Milton however chooses a later version according to which Cassiopeia boasted of her own beauty.

22. Milton invents a pedigree for Melancholy corresponding to that for Mirth.

23. *Vesta* was the goddess of the hearth, and also typified chastity. She was the daughter of Saturn.

24. *solitary Saturn.* Saturn is the most distant of the planets, hence seems solitary. Those born under Saturn were 'melancholy'—*i.e.*, serious-minded, quiet, and unsociable.

25. *in Saturn's reign:* in the Golden Age. See note on *Nativity Ode* (135). Saturn ruled during the Golden Age, until he was overthrown by Jove.

29. *Ida.* A mountain in Crete, the dwelling of Kronos (Saturn).

31. *Nun,* because Melancholy has the virtues of chastity and asceticism.

32. *demure,* solemn. *Cf.* "the drums Demurely wake the sleepers." Shakespeare, *Antony and Cleopatra* (IV, ix, 30).

33. *grain,* dye, or colour.

35. *stole.* A long robe. *Cf.* "sable-stolèd," *Nativity Ode* (220). It could also be used of a hood or veil, and here probably means some kind of scarf or wrap, since a "robe" has already been mentioned.

35. *cipres lawn.* 'Lawn' was a fine transparent material. The spellings 'Cyprus,' 'Cipres,' and 'Cypress' all occur, the first being nearest to the derivation, since the material originally came from Cyprus, as 'cambric' came from Cambrai. 'Cipres' is however more frequent.

36. *decent,* beautiful.

37. *state,* dignity.

39. *commercing,* holding intercourse. Accented on the second syllable; *cf.* "all the commerce that you have had with Troy." Shakespeare, *Troilus and Cressida* (III, iii, 206).

40. *rapt,* transported. From an old verb 'rap,' meaning 'to snatch.'

41. *still*, constantly. *Cf*. "To fetch dew from the still-vex'd Bermoothes." Shakespeare, *The Tempest* (I, ii, 228–229), where "still-vexed" means 'continually tormented by storms.'

42. *Forget thyself to marble.* Milton has the same idea in his *Epitaph on Shakespeare*:

> Then thou, our fancy of itself bereaving,
> Dost make us marble with too much conceiving.

43. *sad*, serious, not necessarily sorrowful.

43. *leaden*, gloomy, because of the colour of lead, and particularly because lead was associated with Saturn. The colour grey, the metal lead, the 'melancholy' person, all were believed to derive their characteristics from the influence of Saturn.

44. *fast*, fixedly—*i.e.*, as steadily as she had previously fixed them on heaven.

47. *Muses:* the goddesses who inspired men with love of the arts. They were called daughters of Jove (Zeus). The Greek poet Hesiod tells how they lived on Mount Helicon and danced round the sacred fountain and the altar of Zeus. Cf. *Lycidas* (15–16):

> Begin then, Sisters of the sacred well,
> That from the seat of Jove doth spring.

54. *The Cherub Contemplation.* See note on *Nativity Ode* (112), on the orders of angels. Each order had its special faculty or characteristic, that of the Cherubim being knowledge and contemplation of divine things.

The chapter in Ezekiel (x) on the throne or chariot surrounded by cherubim evidently impressed Milton, for he alludes to it several times.

Here Milton combines medieval theology with the Old Testament legend, much as he often combines Greek legend with Christian ideas.

55. *hist* probably means 'bring quietly,' and corresponds to "bring" in l. 51.

56. *'Less*, unless.

56. *Philomel:* the nightingale.

56. *deign*, grant.

58. *rugged*, wrinkled.

59. *Cynthia:* Diana, the moon-goddess, so called because she was born on Mount Cynthus in the island of Delos.

59. *dragon yoke.* The moon was imagined as driving a team of dragons.

60. *the accustomed oak:* a tree over which the moon was usually seen to rise by Milton or some other person walking in the country at night.

Note that the 'cheerful man' begins his day at dawn, and hears the song of the lark; the 'thoughtful man' begins his at dusk, and hears the nightingale.

63. *chauntress*, songstress.

65. *unseen.* Contrast "not unseen" in *L'Allegro* (57).

68. *her highest noon:* the highest point in the sky which the moon reaches.

71–72. Cf. *Comus* (331, 333):

> . . . and thou, fair moon . . .
> Stoop thy pale visage through an amber cloud.

73. *plat*, plot.

74. *curfew:* a bell rung at nightfall to warn people to put out their fires, a precaution necessary in the Middle Ages. Until the outbreak of war in 1939 silenced all bells, it was still rung in some places, notably in Cambridge, where Milton must often have heard it. The "wide-watered shore" may be a reminiscence of the fen lands. There are stories of lost travellers in the fens being saved by finding their direction through hearing the curfew bell in Cambridge.

The word 'shore' was often used of the banks of a river, and 'water' is still used of rivers or lakes in some districts— *e.g.*, 'Coniston Water,' 'Derwentwater'—so that "wide-watered shore" would be an apt description of the spreading shallow meres of the fen district. There is no reason why the curfew should be heard especially on the sea-shore.

77. *air*, weather.

78. *still*, quiet.

78. *removèd*, remote.

78. *fit*, suit.

79–80. *I.e.*, the firelight is so dim as almost to be darkness, which 'Il Penseroso' prefers to light.

82. *hearth* was pronounced to rhyme with 'mirth,' as 'earth' still is.

83. *bellman:* the night-watchman, who went the round of every town and village during the night, to keep watch for fires, and guard against criminals, much as the police do now. But he also told the time, reported on the weather, and prayed for God's protection during the night. The well-known carol brings in a bellman's cry—"Past three o'clock, and a cold frosty morning."

83. *charm:* a rhyme, or song, with magic power against evil.

84. *nightly*, by night. Cf. *Nativity Ode* (179), "No nightly trance or breathèd spell.

85–120. Here follow the chief pleasures of the 'thoughtful man,' in particular, reading. We notice that he spends much less time than the 'cheerful man' in country walks, and much more in reading. He also prefers to read plays rather than to see them as 'L'Allegro' does, so also with tournaments.

His reading includes philosophy and theology (85–96), tragedy (97–102), lyric poetry (103–108), and romances (109–120).

87–96. Milton, in common with many men of his day, was a great admirer of Plato, whose philosophy had become more generally known and appreciated in the sixteenth century. Besides Plato's own works, those of the 'neo-Platonists' were studied. The neo-Platonists lived during the early centuries A.D., and adapted Plato's theories to those of their own day. Along with philosophical study some of them were interested in magic, alchemy, and astrology, and in the fourth century they wrote many books on these subjects. These books were attributed to Hermes Trismegistus, and were often referred to and translated, and had great influence throughout the Middle Ages and even in the seventeenth century.

87. *outwatch the Bear. I.e.*, 'sit up all night,' since the constellation of the Bear never sets, but only becomes invisible when the sun rises.

'Il Penseroso' plans to spend the whole night in reading the works of "thrice-great Hermes."

88. *thrice-great Hermes*. The Egyptian god Thoth, who had brought culture and learning to Egypt, was identified with the Greek god Hermes, and called Hermes 'Trismegistus' ('thrice great'). The publication of the books attributed to him caused him to be regarded as the supreme authority on magic, alchemy, astrology, and allied subjects.

88–92. *I.e.*, call down the spirit of Plato from the sphere which it inhabits, to tell where the souls of the dead dwell.

This subject is discussed in Plato's *Phædo* and *Timæus*; in a myth or parable in the latter dialogue Plato suggests that God made as many souls as there are stars, and assigned each soul to a particular star. Those souls which lived a good life on earth returned to their own stars after death to dwell in blessedness. The spirit of Plato himself is to be called from his own star ("unsphere The spirit of Plato"). Cf. *Comus* (2–4):

> . . . where those immortal shapes
> Of bright aerial spirits live insphered
> In regions mild of calm and serene air.

93–96. The doctrine of the demons to be found in fire, air, earth, and water, originated after Plato's time. They were, of course, not 'demons' in the sense in which the word is now often used—of rather petty spiteful creatures—but in the sense of presiding spirits, which were believed to have power over the element proper to them, and over everything in it. There were both good and bad demons.

In *Paradise Regained* (II, 121), Milton represents them as fallen angels, and they are so addressed by Satan:

> "Princes, Heaven's ancient sons, Ethereal Thrones,
> Demonian Spirits now, from the element
> Each of his reign allotted, rightlier called
> Powers of Fire, Air, Water, and Earth beneath."

93. *and of those demons*. *I.e.*, 'and to tell of . . .' implied by "to unfold" (89).

95. *consent*, concord, agreement (the original meaning of the word).

96. *With planet.* The demons were believed to be ruled by the stars, as all other creatures were.

96. *with element.* The 'four elements'—fire, air, earth, and water—were thought to be the materials from which everything was made, and they in turn were governed by their respective demons.

98–102. The 'thoughtful man,' as is to be expected, prefers tragedy (particularly Greek tragedy) to comedy, which the 'cheerful man' chooses.

98. *sceptred*, because Greek tragedies were generally based on the legends of royal families.

98. *pall:* a rich mantle worn by actors in classical drama. Later it came to be used of Church vestments, and of the covering of a coffin.

99. Here follow some of the principal subjects of Greek drama.
Thebes. Æschylus, Sophocles, and Euripides all wrote plays of which the scene is laid in Thebes.
Pelops' line. Especially Agamemnon, Orestes, Iphigenia, and Electra; all three dramatists used these legends.

100. *the tale of Troy.* Euripides wrote several plays on the stories of the events which followed the fall of Troy, as also did Sophocles.
In his preface to *Samson Agonistes* Milton speaks of "Æschylus, Sophocles, and Euripides, the three tragic poets unequalled yet by any, and the best rule to all who endeavour to write tragedy."

102. *buskined, i.e.,* tragic. See note on *L'Allegro* (132).

103. *sad virgin:* Melancholy. "Sad" means 'serious' without the idea of 'sorrow,' as it frequently did at this period.

104. *Musæus.* A Greek seer and poet, sometimes said to be the son of Orpheus. He belongs to the more remote and dim legends of Greek mythology.

104. *bower*, dwelling-place.

105–108. See notes on *L'Allegro* (145–150).

109. *him that left half-told:* Chaucer. The tale is that called *The Squire's Tale*, and tells of the "Tartar King" Cambuscan (Cambyuskan), his sons Algarsyf and Cambalo, and his daughter Canace. An unknown knight presented her with

a "magic ring," which enabled its owner to understand what the birds say, and a mirror which showed the future; he gave to the king a "wondrous horse of brass," which could carry its rider to any place he wished within a day, regardless of distance, and could also fly. Chaucer never finished this tale.

113. *virtuous*, endowed with 'virtue,' that is to say special power. Cf. *Comus* (621), "every virtuous plant."

116–120. This refers to medieval romances in general, including the works of the Italian poets Tasso and Ariosto, which Milton knew. These poems were allegorical—"where more is meant than meets the ear." But no doubt Milton is here thinking particularly of Spenser, for whom he had a very great admiration, and whose *Fairy Queen* is well described by these lines.

118. *trophies hung*. Trophies (the weapons and armour of the defeated) used to be hung up in temples as a dedication to the gods in classical times, and the custom continued during the Middle Ages.

121. *career*. A word regularly used for the courses of the sun and other heavenly bodies.

122. *civil-suited*, soberly dressed, in subdued colours unlike the bright colours of military uniforms in those days. This is a very different dawn from that described in *L'Allegro* (61–62).

123. *tricked*, adorned, decked out.

123. *frounced*, with curled hair.

124. *the Attic boy:* Cephalus, grandson of Cecrops, King of Athens. Eos (the Dawn) saw him as he was hunting, and fell in love with him.

125. *kerchiefed*, wearing a cloud as a scarf or veil over the head, rather like the sun in the *Nativity Ode* (229):

> . . . the sun in bed,
> Curtained with cloudy red.

127. *still*, gentle, soft.

128. *his*. Milton nearly always uses this form of the neuter, rather than 'its,' which was coming into regular use at this time.

130. *minute-drops:* drops falling at regular intervals (of a minute). *Cf.* 'minute-gun.'

   Notice how this vivid description of the shower first falling softly, then ending with the bigger, slow drops as the water collects on the eaves, contrasts with the fanciful description of the dawn just before, and with the formal mythological tone of much of the poem.

131–132. *the sun begins to fling His flaring beams.* A different view is taken of the sunrise by the 'cheerful man':

> . . . the great Sun begins his state,
> Robed in flames and amber light

though some of the same words are used.

134. *brown,* dark.

134. *Sylvan.* Silvanus, or Syɪvanus, was the Roman god of woods and fields, sometimes regarded as the same as Pan, god of nature in general.

135. *monumental* refers to the size and strength of the oak, and also to its quality of monument (or memorial) of events and scenes which have taken place under its shade.

141. *day's . . . eye:* the sun, often called by the Elizabethans "the eye of heaven."

141. *garish.* Juliet takes the same view: "pay no worship to the garish sun." Shakespeare, *Romeo and Juliet* (III, ii, 25). So above (132) the 'thoughtful man' dislikes the "flaring beams" of the sun.

142–146. In Spenser's *Fairy Queen* (I, i, 41) Morpheus is lulled to sleep by trickling water, drizzling rain, and a murmuring wind which sounds like swarming bees.

   Notice the sleepy effect given by these lines.

145. *consort,* harmony. Cf. *Nativity Ode* (132).

146. *dewy-feathered.* In Virgil (*Æneid*, V, 854) Sleep sprinkles dew from a branch on the eyes of Palinurus.

147–150. The exact meaning of this passage is difficult to make out. The general sense seems to be 'May some mysterious dream flutter along ("wave") close to the wings of Sleep, showing itself in a stream of life-like pictures.'

   Milton seems here to have in mind some lines from Jonson's

Vision of Delight, though he does not exactly borrow from them—they seem to be rather in the background of his thought.

> Break, Phant'sie, from thy cave of cloud,
>   And spread thy purple wings;
> Now all thy figures are allowed,
>   And various shapes of things;
> Create of airy forms a stream,
> It must have blood, and nought of phlegm;
> And though it be a waking dream,
>   Yet let it like an odour rise
>   To all the senses here,
>   And fall like sleep upon their eyes,
>   Or music in their ear.

148. *his wings:* the wings of Sleep, recalling "dewy-feathered."

148. *stream* suggests dropping like dew.

149. *lively*, life-like, vivid.

151–152. The same sort of music is heard by Ferdinand in Shakespeare's *Tempest* (I, ii, 385):

> Where should this music be? i'th'air, or th'earth?
> It sounds no more.

153. *some spirit*, like the Attendant Spirit in *Arcades*, who guards "mortals good" from harm.

154. *Genius of the wood*. In *Arcades* the Genius of the Wood has as his chief duty to look after the wood and everything in it, but he is also a musician.

156. *the studious cloisters pale*. This is the reading of the original editions, "pale" meaning 'dim,' as in l. 121: "Thus night oft see me in thy pale career." Most editors now print 'cloister's,' "pale" then being a noun and meaning 'enclosure.'

157. *high embowèd*, arched. Cf. *Comus* (1015), "the bowed welkin."

158. *antic*, quaintly carved. This is really the same word as 'antique,' and the two meanings 'quaint' and 'old' existed side by side. Both forms of the word had the accent on the first syllable.

158. *massy proof*. Several explanations of this phrase are

suggested: (i) 'Safe,' or proof against destruction, because of their massiveness. (ii) Inserting a hyphen, as "star-proof," *Arcades* (89), the meaning then being, 'able to carry the weight above them.'

159. *storied windows:* windows of stained glass in which scenes from sacred story were represented.

161. *organ.* Milton himself played the organ, and often refers to the instrument.

164. *As,* so that it. Cf. *Nativity Ode* (98).

155–166. This passage may well refer to Milton's time at Cambridge; the "studious cloisters" are those of a college, not of a monastery; "high embowèd roof" and "storied windows" well describe the fan-vaulted roof and wonderful stained-glass windows of King's College Chapel, where the services too are such as Milton here describes. But, of course, the descriptions would fit other places too.

When he wrote these lines Milton was still in sympathy with the Established Church and its ritual. Later he took a very different view, and poured scorn on "the singing men and the organs," "the gaudy copes and painted windows" in the Royal Chapel, *Eikonoklastes* (XXIV and XXV).

167. *my weary age.* 'Il Penseroso' has thought of his old age, whereas 'L'Allegro' does not consider it.

170. *spell,* read, study.

171. *of every star.* The key to all knowledge, since the destiny of everything was believed to be controlled by the stars.

171. *shew.* Rhyming with "dew," as with "hue" in *Comus* (994–995).

Arcades

See Introduction, Section IV.

Title. 'The Arcadians.' Arcadia was one of the ancient Greek
states, and lay in mountainous and remote country in the
centre of the Peloponnese. Its inhabitants were mostly
shepherds and hunters, and were considered simple and
backward people. In Renaissance times 'Arcady' was
represented as the home of the conventional shepherds and
shepherdesses who were the subject of 'pastoral' literature,
such as Sidney's *Arcadia.*

Stage directions:

presented to, played before.

habit, dress. Cf. *Comus* (157). We still speak of a monk's
'habit,' and a 'riding-habit.'

seat of state: a throne on a raised platform, here for the
Countess.

    The Countess is seated facing the stage, and the actors
speak directly to her—just as in *Comus* the Attendant
Spirit presents the three children who are taking part in the
masque to their parents. This was a very frequent proceeding in masques.

1. *Nymphs and Shepherds:* the 'Arcades' or 'Arcadians.'

4. *mistook.* We should now say 'mistaken.' The forms were
not sharply distinguished in Milton's day. *Cf.* 'wove' for
'woven' (47).

6. *vows,* prayers, or desires, its Latin meaning.

9. *erst,* formerly, until now.

8–10. The Countess was famous in her day for her beauty and
noble character. Many poets had written poems in her
honour, notably Spenser, who was a distant relative.

14. *state,* magnificence.

16. *silver threads:* perhaps imaginary rays, or they may have

been actual silver stripes in the canopy over the throne. In Spenser's *Fairy Queen* (V, ix, 28) the queen's throne has a "cloth of state" (canopy) over it, "here and there shooting forth silver streams."

20. *Latona:* mother of Apollo, god of the sun, and of Diana, goddess of the moon.

21. *Cybele:* an Asiatic goddess, called 'Mother of the Gods.' The Greeks identified her with Rhea, mother of the Olympian gods. She was said to have taught men to build cities, hence wears a crown of towers.

The Countess had many near relations besides her children and grandchildren. This verse is a compliment to her and to them.

23. *Juno:* queen of the gods.

23. *odds:* allowance made to a weaker player. The line means that Juno dare not compete on equal terms with her—*e.g.*, by giving up the advantage of being a goddess.

24. *clime,* region. Cf. *Comus* (977).

Stage directions:

Genius of the Wood. In *Il Penseroso* (154) Milton hopes to hear music sent by "the unseen Genius of the wood." The Romans believed that every place and person had a special spirit ('genius') to watch over it. Cf. *Nativity Ode* (186).

Probably Henry Lawes, the musician, who played the part of the Attendant Spirit in *Comus*, took this part, which ends with a song, for which he would be specially fitted.

26. *gentle swains.* These were 'swains' (country folk) in appearance, but actually members of the Countess's family, and so "gentle" in the sense of 'well-born.' Cf. *Comus* (236).

26. *for* explains "gentle." The Genius recognizes the "swains" as noblemen because he can see the signs of nobility ("honour") in their faces.

30. *Alpheus:* the god of the river Alpheus which flows through Arcadia. He fell in love with the fountain-nymph Arethusa, who fled from him to Sicily where she reappeared at Syracuse as a spring which still bubbles up close beside the sea and partly actually in it. Alpheus followed, and joined her

there. The river Alpheus disappears and flows underground for some distance, which gave probability to the story.

30. *secret sluice*, underground channel.

32. *breathing* may here mean 'living,' 'in human form,' or perhaps 'sweet-scented.'

33. *silver-buskined*. Diana and her attendant nymphs wore buskins (boots) since they were huntresses.

33. *Nymphs:* the ladies acting in the play, who were dressed as Diana's nymphs.

33. *as great and good. I.e.*, as their companions the "swains."

34. *free intent*, noble purpose.

39. *solemnity*, festival, its Latin meaning. Cf. *Comus* (142).

41. A repetition of the idea in l. 12.

44. *lot*, appointment.

47. *quaint*, elaborate. See note on *Nativity Ode* (194).

47. *wanton*, loose. *Cf.* "wanton ringlets," *Paradise Lost* (IV, 306).

47. *wove*, woven. See note on l. 4.

51. *thwarting*, zig-zag, or going across, or perhaps harmful.

51. *thunder* includes lightning.

52. *cross*, not 'bad-tempered,' but 'slanting'; so in the *Epitaphium Damonis* (80), Milton speaks of Saturn smiting the heart with his slanting leaden shaft. And *cf.* "cross blue lightning," Shakespeare, *Julius Cæsar* (I, iii, 50).

52. *dire-looking*. The stars shed their influence by their gaze. See note on *Nativity Ode* (71).

52. *planet:* Saturn, which was always regarded as malign ("dire-looking").

52. *smites*, *Cf.* Shakespeare, *Hamlet* (I, i, 162)—of Christmas time—"then no planets strike."

53. *cankered*, causing canker (disease).

54. *fetch*, take.

57. *tasselled horn:* a huntsman's horn, decorated with tassels.

56–58. Cf. *L'Allegro* (53–54).

59. *ranks. I.e.*, lines of trees, which the Genius counts as a general would count his soldiers.

60. *puissant*, with magic power.

60. *murmurs*, spells. Cf. *Comus* (526).

61. *else*, at other times.

63–73. See Appendix.

This passage is derived from Plato. In the "Vision of Er," *Republic* (X. 616–617), he describes in a myth or story the vision of the universe seen by certain souls after death. Necessity held in her lap a spindle of adamant, which passed through eight spheres, one enclosed in another like a set of boxes. Her daughters, the Fates (Lachesis, Clotho, and Atropos), were seated at equal intervals from her, and helped to turn the spindle and the spheres through which it passed. On each sphere a siren was seated, singing continually a single note, the eight making up the harmony which was summed up in the ninth sphere. The Fates also sang, in harmony with the notes of the sirens. They also drew from the spindle and spun a thread which represented the life of every human being; this was cut by Atropos when each life should end.

See note on *Nativity Ode* (93–148).

64. *infolded*, one enclosed within the other.

65. *those that hold the vital shears:* the Fates—though, strictly speaking, only one of them held the shears. There is the same reference in *Lycidas* (75–76).

65. *vital* because the shears cut the thread of life.

71. *measured*, in conformity with the music, rhythmical.

73. *mould*, form, or substance. See note on *Nativity Ode* (138).

The Genius, being more than human, can hear the music which men cannot hear, because their ears are "gross." So in Shakespeare, *Merchant of Venice* (V, i, 64), Lorenzo, speaking of the celestial music, adds

> But while this muddy vesture of decay
> Doth grossly close it in, we cannot hear it.

The idea of sin preventing man from hearing the music is not in Plato, but is a Christian addition. Milton puts it forward also in his *Second Prolusion* (see Appendix).

74–76. A high compliment to the Countess—only the music of the spheres is really able to celebrate her as she deserves.

74. *blaze*, proclaim.

76. *Whose lustre leads us.* I.e., the Countess's fame is in the foremost rank.

76. *most fit.* I.e., the music of the spheres is most fit for her.

77. *hit,* be equal to. Cf. *Il Penseroso* (14), *Comus* (286).

78. *go.* I.e., in the procession towards the Countess's throne.

79. *lesser gods,* such as the Genius.

80. *assay,* attempt, essay.

81. *state* here probably means 'throne.'

82. *stem,* stock, family.

84. *enamelled* may suggest the smoothness and brightness of the lawn, but seems also to be rather vaguely used—*e.g.,* in *Paradise Lost* (IV, 149), "gay enamelled colours."

There must have been an interval between the two songs, filled by a dance of the Nymphs and Shepherds.

97. *Ladon:* a river in Arcadia.

98–102. *Lycæus, Cyllene, Erymanthus,* and *Mænalus* are mountains in Arcadia, Erymanthus being the name of a river also. Pan was said to be specially fond of Lycæus and Mænalus.

106. *Syrinx:* daughter of the river-god Ladon. Pan pursued her, and she was changed into a reed, from which he made a pipe ('pan-pipes').

108–109. The last two lines of the first song repeated, after the Nymphs and Shepherds have themselves seen the Countess.

Comus

See Introduction, Section IV.

Stage directions:

Presented, acted.

The Attendant Spirit descends or enters. In two manuscripts the Attendant Spirit is called "A Guardian Spirit, or Daemon." Such dæmons are different from the dæmons who live in and rule the elements—see note on *Il Penseroso* (93). They are identified with the Christian Guardian Angels.

descends implies stage mechanism.

2. *mansion*, dwelling-place. Cf. *Il Penseroso* (92); but there is also a reference to the "many mansions" of St John (xiv, 2).

2. *those.* I.e., those well-known. Cf. *Lycidas* (130), "that two-handed engine."

insphered. See note on *Il Penseroso* (88–92).

4. *In regions mild*, like the heaven of the Greek gods, where there was no wind, rain, or snow, but always sun and fair weather—Homer, *Odyssey* (VI, 43–44).

4. *serene.* Scanned as 'sérene.'

5. A reminiscence of Horace, *Odes* (III, xxix, 12), who advises his friend to avoid "the smoke and display and noise of Rome." Perhaps Milton had London in mind.

6. *low-thoughted.* I.e., concerned with material instead of spiritual things.

6–11. "Men," which first appears in a subordinate clause, is the subject of the principal clause which follows.

7. *pestered*, clogged, hence 'crowded.'

7. *pinfold*, pound, or enclosure for strayed animals.

10. *mortal change:* death. Cf. *Paradise Lost* (X, 272), "the smell Of mortal change on earth."

11. *enthron'd gods on sainted seats.* Milton is thinking both of the Greek gods on their thrones on Olympus, and also of the four-and-twenty seats of the elders in Revelation (iv, 4).

16. *ambrosial,* immortal, heavenly.

16. *weeds,* garments. See note on *L'Allegro* (120).

17. *mould.* See note on *Nativity Ode* (138). The Spirit has assumed human form.

20. *high and nether Jove.* After overthrowing Saturn, Zeus ("high Jove") took the sky, Poseidon (Neptune) the sea, and Hades (Pluto, "nether Jove") the underworld as their respective domains.

22–23. Very like the description of England, "This precious stone set in the silver sea," by John of Gaunt, in Shakespeare, *Richard II* (II, i, 46).

23. *unadornèd,* without any other adornment.

25. *By course,* duly.

25. *several:* each to its special ruler.

26. *sapphire,* blue, to suit a sea-god.

27. *their little tridents.* They are after all of inferior rank, so have only "little" tridents. The three-pronged trident was the sceptre of Neptune.

28. *main,* sea.

29. *quarters to,* assigns to.

29. *blue-haired.* The idea of blue-haired sea-gods is primarily classical, but they were frequently so shown in masques.

30. *this tract. I.e.,* Wales, and the counties bordering upon it.

30. *that fronts the falling sun.* To the west.

31. *a noble peer:* the Earl of Bridgewater. A sudden change from the mythological gods to a real person actually present at the performance.

33. *nation:* the Welsh.

33. *proud in arms.* A translation of Virgil's epithet for the Romans, *Æneid* (I, 21). The Welsh claimed to be descended from the Romans, so this is a tactful compliment to them.

34. *his fair offspring:* the three children who were actually taking part in the play.

35. *attend,* be in attendance on.

35. *state:* his installation as Lord President of Wales, at Ludlow

37. *perplexed*, intricate, tangled. The accent is on the first syllable.

37. *this drear wood*. This wood is one of the

> . . . forests, and enchantments drear,
> Where more is meant than meets the ear.
>
> (*Il Penseroso*, 119)

See Introduction, p. 36.

Milton now takes us from the classical world into the world of medieval romance and magic (though we shall still find many classical allusions).

38. *horror*. See Note on *Nativity Ode* (172).

39. *forlorn*, lost.

44. *What never yet was heard*. A claim often made by poets, as by Milton himself again in *Paradise Lost* (I, 14–16). It is a frequent way of beginning in the old romances.

45. *hall or bower*. The hall was the chief room of a castle or large house, the bower the inner or ladies' apartment. The two words together were a stock phrase of the old romances. Chaucer makes fun of it in the "Nun's Priest's Tale" (4022), where, speaking of a poor widow, he says, "Full sooty was her bower and eke her hall."

46. *Bacchus:* the god of wine.

48. *after the Tuscan mariners transformed*. A Latin way of speaking, where we should now say 'after the transformation of the Tuscan mariners.' So in *Paradise Lost* (I, 573) Milton writes "never since created man," instead of 'since the creation of man.'

The legend of the "Tuscan mariners" was that Bacchus was captured by Italian ("Tuscan") pirates, but turned their ship into an arbour of vines and themselves into dolphins.

49. *Tyrrhene shore:* the coast of Etruria (Tuscania).

49. *listed*, willed.

50. *Circe:* daughter of Helios (the Sun). Homer (*Odyssey*, X) tells how Odysseus was wrecked on her island, and his companions turned into swine. She is the original enchantress of romance.

50. *fell*, came upon.

55. *with ivy berries wreathed*. *Cf.* "ivy-crownèd Bacchus."

L'Allegro (16). Bacchus was traditionally represented with garlands of vine and ivy.

56. *parted*, departed.

57. *Much like his father*, in loving sensual pleasures.

57. *but his mother more*, in his charm and beauty, and as having the power of sorcery.

58. *Comus.* The word means dance, or revel. Jonson used the name for his god of revelry.

59. *frolic*, gay.

60. *Celtic and Iberian fields:* France and Spain.

61. *this:* the wood shown on the stage.

61. *ominous*, full of portents.

65. *orient*, bright.

66. *the drouth of Phœbus:* thirst caused by the heat of the sun.

67. *fond*, foolish. Cf. *Il Penseroso* (6).

69. *express*, exact.

A reference to Genesis (i, 27): "God created man in his own image."

71. *ounce*, lynx, or some such animal.

73. *misery*, misfortune.

76. In Homer the men transformed into swine by Circe still retain their human minds, and are aware of what has happened to them. But Milton makes the people transformed by Comus quite unaware of it, thus suggesting the completeness of Comus's power.

79. *adventurous*, full of adventures.

80. *glancing star.* Notice how the sound of the line suggests the swiftness of the star's passage.

83. *Iris:* the rainbow. So in *Paradise Lost* (XI, 244), "Iris had dipped the woof" of the Archangel Michael's garment.

87. *knows to*, knows how to, a Latin form of speech.

86–88. A compliment to Lawes (to be spoken by himself). A similar compliment is paid to him (in the guise of the "swain" Thyrsis) in ll. 494–496. He was at the time music-master to the Earl of Bridgewater's family, so "to the service of the house belongs."

88. *nor of less faith*, and as trustworthy (as he is musical).

89. *office*, duty.

90. *likeliest*, fittest.

90. *nearest the present aid. I.e.*, 'nearest at hand to help as may be needed.'

92. *viewless*, invisible.

Stage directions:

    rout, rabble, drove.

    headed like, with heads like.

93. *Comus*. In Ben Jonson's masque Comus is the jovial, gross leader of the revellers, as indeed his name suggests. But Milton's Comus is very different. He has great charm (as his mother Circe has in the stories about her), and some of the most beautiful poetry is put into his mouth. Nor is he the terrifying magician of medieval tales. Milton does not divide everything into black or white, but allows their value to worldly delights, though virtue triumphs in the end.

93. *The star:* Venus, or Hesperus, the Evening Star.

93. *bids the shepherd fold. I.e.*, whose rising is the sign for the shepherd to shut up his sheep in the fold.

96. *allay*, cool. The wheels of the sun's chariot become so hot that the sea hisses as they touch it, according to classical poets.

97. *Atlantic stream:* the stream of Ocean, which encircled the earth, according to ancient theories. The sun was believed to sink into it when setting, and to be carried round its northern half to rise again in the east.

98–99. The sun lights up the north pole on his journey to the east.

105. *rosy twine*, wreaths of roses.

110. *saws*, sayings, maxims. *Cf.* "full of wise saws and modern instances" (of the Justice). Shakespeare, *As You Like It* (II, vii, 156).

111. *fire*, of which spirits were made, whereas mortals were made of earthly mould. (See l. 17).

113. *watchful spheres.* Cf. *Nativity Ode* (21).

114. *round*, dance.

113–114. See Appendix.

    The movements of the spheres are represented as a dance, *e.g.*, in *Paradise Lost* (V, 620–627).

months and years. Genesis (i, 14): "And God said, Let there be lights in the firmament . . . and let them be for signs, and for seasons, and for days, and years." Here again Milton combines the accepted theology with classical theories.

115. *sounds*, straits of the sea.

116. *to the moon*, in obedience to the moon.

116. *morrice*. A folk-dance. The tides are represented as a dance of the seas, led by the moon.

118. *pert*, brisk, lively.

121. *wakes*. Strictly speaking, religious festivals held at night. Comus uses the word for revels at night.

123. *prove*, try.

127. *dun*, dusky.

128. *Cotytto:* a Thracian goddess whose rites were held by night, and had an evil reputation in ancient times.

132. *Stygian darkness*, darkness like that through which the river Styx flowed in Hades.

132. *spets*, spits out.

134. *ebon*, black as ebony.

135. *Hecat':* a goddess of night, and so associated with Cotytto. She was also the goddess of magic and of the witches.

137. *dues*, rites proper to her.

138. *blabbing*, tell-tale. So Shakespeare has "the gaudy, blabbing and remorseful day." *2 Henry VI* (IV, i, 1).

139. *nice*. A word which used to have a meaning, and now has practically none. It used to mean precise, fastidious, fussy; here perhaps suggesting that Morn would disapprove of their behaviour.

139. *Indian*, for 'Eastern' in general.

140. *cabined*, narrow, confined.

140. *peep*. Often used of dawn. We still say 'at peep of dawn.'

141. *descry*, reveal.

142. *solemnity*, festival. *Cf.* note on *Arcades* (39).

144. *fantastic*. *Cf.* "light fantastic toe," *L'Allegro* (34).

The Measure. This was properly a stately kind of dance, but Comus's name for it, "round," is probably a better description, since the stage directions in the acting version say "The Measure, in a wild, rude, and wanton antick."

145. *Break off.* *Sc.* from the dance.

147. *shrouds,* hiding-places. Cf. *Nativity Ode* (218): "Nought but profoundest hell can be his shroud."

147. *brakes,* thickets.

151. *trains,* lures, enticements.

153. *thus.* Comus throws some fine dust.

154. *dazzling.* Milton originally wrote "powdered," and had evidently forgotten the alteration when he wrote "this magic dust" in l. 165.

154. *spongy,* moist, hence more apt to cause mists and illusions.

155. *blear,* misty.

156. *presentments,* appearances.

157. *quaint habits,* strange dress. See note on stage directions to *Arcades.*

159. *course,* purpose.

161. *glozing:* flattering (with the idea of deceit).

163. *wind me. I.e.,* insinuate myself into his trust.

163. *easy-hearted,* unsuspicious.

165. *virtue,* power, as in Canace's "virtuous ring and glass." *Il Penseroso* (113).

167. *gear,* business, affairs. The word usually meant the tools of a trade, as it does now.

168. *fairly,* quietly.

174. *hinds,* peasants.

175. *teeming,* breeding.

175. *granges,* barns.

176. *Pan.* See note on *Nativity Ode* (89).

178. *swilled,* drunken.

180. *inform,* direct. *Cf.* Milton, *Samson Agonistes* (335):

> "My son, now captive, hither hath informed
> Your younger feet."

184. *favour,* protection.

189. *sad,* serious. Cf. *Il Penseroso* (103), "sad virgin."

189. *votarist,* a person under a religious vow.

189. *palmer,* pilgrim. Those who had been on pilgrimage to the Holy Land carried a palm-branch in token of it.

196. *felonious,* carrying on the idea of "had stole them."

197. *in thy dark lantern.* Night is a burglar, who shuts up the dark lantern in which the stars are (namely the whole sky), so causing darkness.

The passage (ll. 194–200) is an example of the 'conceits' which the taste of the time approved, but which seem rather absurd to us—the picture of the sun in bed in the *Nativity Ode* is a more extreme instance. The suggestion that the only reason for the darkness of the night is that the Lady's brothers might be stolen from her is far-fetched, and the idea that the only purpose of the stars is to light the traveller is almost equally so; Milton himself ridiculed the idea in his *Seventh Prolusion*, when he says:

Can we indeed believe that the vast spaces of boundless air are illuminated and adorned with everlasting lights, that they are endowed with such rapidity of motion and pass through such intricate revolutions, merely to serve as a lantern for base and slothful men, and to light the path of the idle and the sluggard here below?

Warton, an eighteenth-century commentator, has however a useful reminder to those who condemn these oddities. He says:

In the present age, in which almost every common writer avoids palpable absurdities . . . would Milton have introduced this passage, when thievish Night is supposed, for some felonious purpose, to shut up the stars in her dark lantern? Certainly not. But in the present age, correct and rational as it is, had *Comus* been written, we should not perhaps have had some of the greatest beauties of its wild and romantic imagery.

201–209. See Introduction, p. 35.

203. *rife*, plentiful.

203. *perfect*, distinct. *Cf.* l. 73, "so perfect is their misery."

204. *single*, only. *Cf.* l. 369, "the single want of light and noise." ('Only the lack of,' 'the mere lack of.')

212. *siding*, accompanying.

212. *Conscience.* Three syllables.

216. *I see ye visibly.* Plato held that if any man could actually see the ideal Good he would necessarily adore and follow it.

217. *supreme.* Accented on the first syllable.

221–224. The repetition of words strikes us as odd, but was admired in Milton's time. A much longer and more elaborate example is to be found in *Paradise Lost* (IV, 641–656), where the length and detail make it less startling to us than the quick repetition here.

230. *Echo:* a mountain nymph who fell in love with Narcissus, the son of a river-god. Her love not being returned, she pined away until only her voice remained. Narcissus, who had fallen in love with his own reflection, was changed into the flower called after him.

231. *airy shell.* This is sometimes taken to mean the vault of the sky, but this explanation does not suit the following lines. It is better to take the "shell" as a cavern, the usual haunt of Echo. (The manuscript gives "cell," which indicates what was in Milton's mind.)

232. *Meander:* a river in Asia Minor. It has many twists and turns, so has given us the verb 'to meander.'

232. *margent,* margin, edge.

235. *sad,* here in its usual meaning.

236. *gentle,* of noble birth.

241. *Parley,* dialogue, as Echo seems to reply.

241. *Daughter of the Sphere.* Cf. Milton, *At a Solemn Music* (2), "Sphere-born harmonious sisters, Voice and Verse." Echo is represented as springing from the music of the spheres. (See Appendix.)

242. *translated,* removed (to a higher place).

243. *resounding,* sounding again, as an echo does.

244–248. Milton expresses the same idea in his Latin poem, *To Leonora Singing,* when he says that the music of her voice shows the presence of God himself, or of some divine agency working through her.

248. *his,* its.

249. *they,* the raptures.

251. *fall,* cadence.

252. *it,* darkness.

251. *the raven down Of darkness.* I.e., darkness, black as the raven's down. For the comparison of darkness to a black bird cf. *L'Allegro* (6, 7).

253. *Sirens* were said to live on an island not far from Scylla, in the straits between Italy and Sicily. By their song they so captivated sailors that they forgot their duties and allowed their boats to be wrecked on the island.

254. *flowery-kirtled*. A kirtle is a sort of tunic.

254. *Naiades:* nymphs of streams and springs.

256. *take the prisoned soul.* *I.e.*, 'take the soul prisoner,' (a Latin construction).

257. *Elysium:* a happiness like that enjoyed by souls in Elysium. See note on *L'Allegro* (147).

257. *Scylla:* a monster living on the Italian side of the straits separating Sicily from Italy. She had a woman's body, a fish's tail, and several heads, and barked like a dog. Scylla caught and devoured sailors wrecked on her shore.

257. *Charybdis:* a monster living on the opposite shore to Scylla, which alternately sucked in and spat out the waters of the strait in a whirlpool.

260–264. Circe and her companions could only lull the senses to sleep, whereas the Lady's song made them more acute.

267. *Unless the goddess.* *I.e.*, 'you were certainly never born in this place, unless you are the goddess who rules over it.'

268. *Pan* is here the pagan god of nature without any of the Christian symbolism such as we find in *Nativity Ode* (89).

269–270. Comus attributes to the Lady the power exercised by the Genius of the Wood in *Arcades* (48–50).

271. *gentle shepherd.* The Lady takes Comus for a peasant, as he said she would by the action of the "magic dust" (165).

273. *boast of skill*, boastful wish to show skill.

273. *extreme shift*, last resort. *Cf.* "care and utmost shifts" (617).

277–290. These lines imitate a model often used in Greek tragedy, when two people meet and exchange quick question and answer in alternate lines. This device gives an impression of speed and urgency.

279. *near-ushering*, closely attending.

282. A slightly different reason from the one she gave before. (See l. 186.)

285. *prevented* probably means 'anticipated' ('go before'). *Cf. Nativity Ode* (24), "prevent them with thy humble ode."

This is the more frequent meaning at this period, but here the usual modern sense may be intended.

286. *hit*, guess.

287. *Imports their loss*. I.e., 'Is the loss of them important to you, apart from your present need?' Comus tries tactfully to find out who the "gentle pair" are.

290. *Hebe*. See note on *L'Allegro* (29).

291–292. These two lines have a classical flavour, as the 'unyoking of oxen' is often used by ancient writers to indicate evening. In the next line we are in the English countryside.

292. *loose*. I.e., unfastened from the plough.

293. *swinked*, tired out.

296. *mantling*, covering like a mantle.

297. *port*, deportment, bearing.

298. *vision*. Three syllables.

299. *element*, air.

301. *plighted*, folded, plaited, or interwoven.

312. *Dingle:* a narrow valley between two hills.

312. *bosky bourn*, wooded stream.

315. *stray attendance*, attendants who have strayed—abstract for concrete.

316. *shroud*, are taking shelter. The noun "shroud" occurs in l. 147 in the same sense.

317–318. The lark's nest is on the ground ("low-roosted"), and made of dry grass ("thatched pallet").

318. *pallet:* a bed of straw.

325. *where it first was named*. I.e., from which its name is derived.

327. *warranted*, guarded, protected.

329. *Eye me*, keep watch over me.

329. *square*, measure. We still say 'It does not square with . . .'

331. *Unmuffle*, remove a veil from the face.

332. *benison*, blessing.

333. *Stoop thy pale visage*. Cf. *Il Penseroso* (71–72).

334. *disinherit*, dispossess. 'Inherit' could mean merely 'possess,' without the idea of receiving a legacy. So in the *Book of Common Prayer*, "Bless thine inheritance."

334. *Chaos* is (1) the confused mass of matter which was believed to have existed before it was brought into order and

formed into the world, (2) the god who ruled over it. Milton makes Night and Chaos preside over the primeval darkness in *Paradise Lost* (II, 894–910).

335. *double night.* I.e., the darkness of the wood made darker still by night. Cf. *Paradise Regained* (I, 499):

> . . . for now began
> Night with her sullen wing to double-shade
> The desert.

336. *influence.* See note on *Nativity Ode* (71).

338. *the wicker hole:* the hole (serving for a window) in some hut of wattle and daub—"wicker . . . clay."

340. See Introduction, p. 38.

341. *star of Arcady:* Callisto, daughter of Lycaon, king of Arcadia, was changed into the constellation of the Great Bear, and her son Arcas into the Little Bear, or Arcturus. The Greeks navigated by the Great Bear, the Phœnicians (Tyrians) by the Pole Star (Cynosura), which forms the tail of the Lesser Bear.

See note on *L'Allegro* (80).

342. Giving up hope of seeing anything in the darkness, the Second Brother seeks a clue through hearing.

344. *wattled cotes:* sheepfolds made of hurdles.

345. *pastoral reed.* The pipe made of oat or reed stems is that used by shepherds in pastoral poetry.

345. *stops:* the holes in the pipe which produce the different notes.

346. *lodge:* hut (in the forest). Still used in this sense in the phrase 'hunting lodge.'

347. *his feathery dames.* Like the cock in *L'Allegro* (52), who "Stoutly struts his dames before."

349. *innumerous,* innumerable.

351. Notice the effect of the *w* and *wh* sounds, as of whispering voices.

359. *exquisite,* inquisitive, curious.

360. *cast,* foretell. *Cf.* 'to cast a horoscope.'

360. *fashion,* nature.

365. *delusion.* Four syllables.

366. *to seek*, at a loss.

367. *unprincipled*, ignorant of the principles.

368. *bosoms*, keeps in its bosom.

369. *single*, mere, only. *Cf.* note on l. 204.

373. *Cf.* "Virtue gives herself light, through darkness for to wade" (Spenser, *Fairy Queen*, I, i, 12), spoken by the Red Cross Knight to Una, lost in the wood.

375. *the flat sea. Cf.* "the level brine," *Lycidas* (98).

376. *seeks to*, resorts to. So often in the Authorized Version of the Old Testament.

377. *Contemplation.* Five syllables.

378. *plumes*, preens.

379. *resort*, crowds.

380. *all to-ruffled.* This may be read in two ways:
   (1) "all-to" meaning entirely.
   (2) "to-ruffled" meaning ruffled up. This is probably the correct explanation, and suits the run of the line better.

382. *the centre. Sc.* 'of the earth,' a frequent omission.

385. *his own dungeon. Cf.* Milton, *Samson Agonistes* (155–156), "Thou art become . . . The dungeon of thyself."

385–392. Cf. *Il Penseroso* (167–172).

386. *affects*, loves.

389. *senate-house:* the Curia, where the Senate or governing body of Rome met.

391. *beads*, rosary.

393. *Hesperian tree.* There are several versions of the story of the Hesperides, and Milton uses that current at the time, according to which there were three Hesperides, daughters of Hesperus. They had a garden somewhere in North Africa, in which grew the tree which bore golden apples, entrusted to their care by Hera. It was also guarded by a dragon which had a hundred heads, some of which were always awake. One of the tasks set to Heracles was to obtain the golden apples.

   Milton speaks of the Hesperides again (981–983).

394–395. *had need . . . watch*, needs a dragon to keep watch over her.

395. *unenchanted*, not to be enchanted. See note on *L'Allegro* (40).

398. *unsunned*, kept in the dark, hidden.

401. *Danger*, power over a person. This is actually the original meaning.

401. *wink on*, shut the eye to.

407. *unownèd*, unaccompanied.

408. *Infer as if*, conclude that.

409. *without*, beyond.

410. *poise*, weight.

411. *arbitrate the event*, determine the outcome.

413. *squint*, looking askance.

419. *if*, even if.

421. *complete*. Accented on the first syllable.

423. *trace*, go to and fro in.

423. *unharboured*, giving no shelter.

426. *mountaineer*. Not 'climbers,' but men living in wild and mountainous places, and therefore likely to be wild themselves.

428. *very*, absolute.

429. *horrid*, bristling (the original meaning), hence 'terrifying'.

430. *unblenched*, undismayed (literally 'not made pale by fear').

431. *Be it not done*, provided it is not done.

433. *fire:* the will-o'-the-wisp, or Jack-o'-lantern. Cf. *L'Allegro* (104).

433. *moorish*, like a moor.

434. *blue*, livid, often applied to witches; for example, Sycorax, Caliban's mother, is called "blue-eyed," Shakespeare, *The Tempest* (I, ii, 269), meaning that she had bluish circles round her eyes, not that she had blue eyes.

434. *hag:* an evil spirit in the form of a woman.

434. *stubborn:* because it refuses to be laid.

434. *unlaid ghost:* spirit whose unatoned sins kept him earthbound.

435. *That breaks his magic chains. I.e.*, gets his freedom. Ghosts and spirits of all sorts could walk about the earth at night, but must return to their proper places at dawn. See note on *Nativity Ode* (231). The curfew is a signal to them that the night has begun, so they welcome it, as the elves in Shakespeare's *Tempest* (V, i, 39–40) "rejoice To hear the solemn curfew." See note on *Il Penseroso* (74).

436. *swart*, dark, black.

436. *fairy of the mine.* Mines were believed to be inhabited by goblins of various sorts, some dangerous, some helpful. Disney's dwarfs in *Snow-White* are their modern counterpart.

439. *schools of Greece:* Greek philosophy. So far the examples have been taken from medieval lore.

440. *testify*, bring as a witness.

442. *silver-shafted.* As goddess of the moon as well as of the chase, Diana has silver arrows.

443. *brinded*, brindled—tawny-coloured and striped.

444. *pard*, leopard.

445. *bolt*, arrow.

447. *What was* . . . Carried on by "but" in l. 450.

447. *snaky-headed Gorgon shield.* The Gorgon Medusa was one of three monstrous sisters. Her face was very beautiful, but she had snakes instead of hair. Whoever looked at her was turned into stone. Perseus was able to kill her through looking at her reflection in a mirror to avoid seeing her actual face. The head of the Gorgon formed the centre of Athene's (Minerva's) shield.

448. *Minerva:* Athene. Her characteristics were wisdom and virginity.

449. *congealed.* Accented on the first syllable. Note the effect of the *f* and *s* sounds to suggest a shiver of cold.

450. *rigid.* With a reference to the power possessed by the Gorgon's head of turning the beholder to stone.

451. *noble grace.* Perhaps suggesting also the famous beauty of Medusa.

452. *blank* may mean 'sheer,' or perhaps 'at a loss,' as Satan was "solicitous and blank"—*i.e.*, troubled and at a loss, in *Paradise Regained* (II, 120).

454. *sincerely*, entirely.

455. *lackey*, attend and guard.

458. *no gross ear can hear.* Cf. *Arcades* (72), of the music of the spheres:

> . . . which none can hear
> Of human mould with gross unpurgèd ear.

459. *oft* is here an adjective.

461. *temple of the mind:* the body.

459–462. In *Paradise Lost* (V, 469–500) Milton works out this
idea in greater detail. The archangel Raphael explains to Adam
how all life is really one, and every kind can be transmuted
into a higher sort, till at last men may become as angels.

468. *Imbodies and imbrutes.* So Satan complains of having to
take the form of the serpent, and being obliged "This essence
to incarnate and imbrute." *Paradise Lost* (IX, 166).

469. *property*, nature.

470. *shadows:* a different kind of ghost from that of l. 434.
Here the spirit cannot be freed from the body because it has
allowed itself to become too closely identified with it, and
does not wish to leave it.

This whole passage (470–475) is closely modelled on Plato's
theories as expressed in the *Phædo*, where Socrates puts
forward the idea that the truly noble soul is glad to be freed
from the body, but the ignoble soul is so attached to the body
and to bodily pleasures that it cannot tear itself away, but
haunts the sepulchre. The idea was taken up by Christian
writers, with emphasis on the evil of the body.

473. *it.* Milton transfers to the singular from the plural
"shadows," and "it" refers to one of the shadows mentioned
in l. 470.

474. *and linked itself*, and which linked itself.

476. *charming.* A stronger expression than it is now—'enchanting.'

476. *divine philosophy:* the philosophy concerned with divine
matters, especially Plato's as set forth in the Elder Brother's
speech.

478. *Apollo's lute.* Apollo was god of music, and is often
represented as playing the lyre. He was also the god of
philosophy.

480. *crude*, undigested.

483. *night-foundered*, overwhelmed by night.

486. *Again, again.* The shout is heard coming nearer and nearer.

486. *draw.* Sc. our swords.

490. *That hallo.* The Elder Brother had shouted (as he said

he would), and the spirit, still unseen, replied. "That hallo" refers to the reply.

491. *iron stakes:* their swords.

494. *Thyrsis.* One of the traditional names for a shepherd. It occurs also in *L'Allegro* (83).

494–496. Another compliment to Lawes.

495–512. Here follows a series of rhymed couplets. The immediate effect of the rhyme is to suggest pastoral poetry, but other important effects are that it relieves the tension of the excitingly dramatic episode which has just occurred, and also leads up to Comus's long speech, which would otherwise follow too closely on the previous dramatic scene.

495. *huddling.* Stopping and crowding together in order to hear the music, as they did for Orpheus. See note on *L'Allegro* (145).

495. *madrigal:* a part-song for voices alone. Lawes was well known as a composer of madrigals.

499. *pent,* penned in the fold.

501. *his next joy:* the younger brother.

502. *toy,* trifle.

503. *stealth,* secret going.

504. *fleecy wealth. I.e.,* sheep.

506. *To,* compared to.

508. *how chance,* how does it happen that.

509. *blame,* fault. Cf. *Nativity Ode* (41).

512. *shew.* The spelling indicates that the word rhymes with "true," in l. 511. *Cf.* ll. 994–995, where "hue" and "shew" rhyme.

516. *Storied,* related.

517. *Chimeras:* a monster with the head of a lion, the body of a goat, and the tail of a serpent.

518. *rifted rocks,* cleft—*i.e.,* caves, which the Greeks very naturally supposed to be the entrance to Hades.

520. *navel,* centre.

526. *murmurs,* murmured spells. Cf. *Arcades* (60), where, however, the spells are good ones.

529–530. *unmoulding . . . face.* Destroying the stamp imprinted on the face by reason.

M

529. *reason:* the essential and highest quality of man according to Plato.

529. *mintage:* stamp or design on a coin.

530. *charactered,* imprinted. Accented "charáctered," as in Shakespeare, *Hamlet* (I, iii, 58):

> . . . these few precepts in thy memory
> Look thou character.

531. *crofts,* small farms.

532. *brow,* overlook.

532. *bottom,* valley.

533. *monstrous rout,* rout of monsters.

534. *stabled* would seem to mean 'in their lairs,' as in *Paradise Lost* (XI, 747), "sea-monsters whelped and stabled." But it may rather be a reminiscence of Virgil, *Eclogues* (III, 80), and mean 'in the sheepfold.' This goes better with "tigers at their prey" than the other meaning.

535. *Hecate.* See note on l. 135.

537. *Yet.* Although they are repulsive, yet they have means of attracting.

539. *unweeting,* unwitting. Milton generally uses this form of the word.

540. *by then,* by the time that.

542. *besprent,* sprinkled.

546. *melancholy.* Not sadness, but quiet contemplation such as that described in *Il Penseroso.*

547. *meditate,* practise. The line comes from Virgil, *Eclogues* (I, 2). Cf. *Lycidas* (66), "strictly meditate the thankless Muse."

548. *close,* cadence, as in *Nativity Ode* (100). Or perhaps merely 'the end of the song.'

551. *listened.* Transitive, as often at this period.

552. *stop of sudden silence.* The point at which Comus broke off the dance (145).

553. *drowsy frighted,* frightened by the noise, although so drowsy.

554. *litter:* a sort of sedan chair in which one could lie down.

554. *close-curtained Sleep.* Like the sun in bed, *Nativity Ode* (230). The same expression—"curtained sleep"—occurs in Shakespeare, *Macbeth* (II, i, 51).

555. Refers to the Lady's song.

557. *that*, so that.

560. *Still to be so displaced*, if her place might always be taken by such music.

560. *Still*, always. *Cf.* note on *Il Penseroso* (41).

562. *the ribs of Death*. The music was so beautiful that it would bring back life into a mere skeleton.

565. *harrowed with*, overcome by.

568. *lawns*, open spaces in the wood. Cf. *Nativity Ode* (85).

573. *prevent*, forestall, arrive first, as in *Nativity Ode* (24).

583. *confidence*, assurance.

585. *period*, sentence.

586. *for me*, as far as I am concerned.

590. *enthralled*, enslaved (thrall = slave).

591. *which mischief meant most harm*, which mischievous men intended to be most harmful.

592. *happy trial*, test which ends happily.

593–597. The evil element gradually separates from the good, and destroys itself.

594. *when*, until.

595. *settled to itself*, sunk down into a mass, like impurities in a liquid, or lees in wine. *Cf.* l. 809.

597. *If this fail*, if this is not true.

598. *The pillared firmament*. Cf. *Paradise Regained* (IV, 455), "the pillared frame of heaven." The expression recalls Job (xxvi, 11): "The pillars of heaven tremble."

602. *for*, as for.

602. *let him be girt*, even if he were girt.

603. *legions*. Three syllables.

604. *Acheron:* one of the rivers of the underworld, here meaning the underworld itself. *Cf.* "Stygian" (132).

605. *Harpies:* great birds with human faces, which carried people off to Hades. In the stories of Phineus and of Æneas the Harpies swoop down and carry off food set out on tables, or make it uneatable.

605. *Hydra:* a serpent-like monster with nine heads, two of which grew when one was cut off. It was destroyed by Heracles.

606. *'Twixt Africa and Ind*. Africa was the farthest west, India ("Ind") the farthest east of the ancient world.

607. *purchase*, prey. The idea of buying is a later one.

610. *yet*, nevertheless (although it is hopeless).

610. *emprise*, adventurous enterprise.

611. *stead*, advantage, service.

614. *his bare wand*, his wand alone.

617. *relation*, report.

617. *utmost shift*. *Cf.* "extreme shifts" (273).

620. *regard*, importance.

620. *see to*, look at.

621. *virtuous*, powerful, especially in magic. *Cf.* note on l. 165.

626. *scrip*, bag.

627. *simples*, remedies, especially herbal ones.

633. Note the extra syllable at the end of the line; *cf.* l. 755.

634. *like esteemed*, unknown, and therefore not valued.

635. *clouted shoon*, hob-nailed boots. This makes better sense here than 'patched shoes,' which is a possible meaning. A contemporary poet, Corbet, has the expression "and leavest such prints on beauty . . . as clouted shoon do on a floor of loam."

636. *moly*. Hermes gave Ulysses a herb called moly, which had a black root and a milk-white flower, and which made Ulysses immune to Circe's poisoned cup.

638. *hæmony*. A name invented by Milton, probably with reference to Hæmonia (Thessaly), a land famed for witchcraft.

639. *sovran*, supreme.

640. *mildew blast*, blight caused by mildew.

640. *damp*, fog, vapour. *Cf.* 'fire-damp' in mines.

641. *Furies*. Not the Furies of Greek mythology, but any evil spirits in female form, such as the "hag" in l. 434.

641. *apparition*. Five syllables.

642. *pursed it up*, stored it up.

642. *little reckoning made*, thought little about it.

646. *lime-twigs*, twigs smeared with sticky material to catch birds.

651. *with brandished blade*. So, in Homer, Hermes bids Ulysses attack Circe with his sword as soon as he has drunk the cup and remained unharmed.

655. *the sons of Vulcan*. Vulcan was the god of fire and of the crafts which make use of it, such as that of the blacksmith. His workshop was under Mount Etna, hence the flames and smoke which burst from the mountain.

Stage directions:
  puts by, refuses.
  goes about, tries.

659–662. See Introduction, pp. 14–16, on this passage.

660. *nerves*, sinews.

660. *alablaster*. The old form of 'alabaster.' Statues were often made of alabaster, and many Elizabethan monuments made of it are to be seen in churches.

661. *Daphne*. See Introduction, Section VII.

662. *Root-bound*, 'or root-bound, as Daphne was.' Milton puts "root-bound" inside the clause, so adding variety and emphasis. Coming where it does, "root-bound" has an almost startling effect.

664. *corporal rind*. The body being, as it were, the shell of the soul.

666. Note the rhythm in this line. It is very dramatic, with a pause between the two questions, and a broken rhythm like that of ordinary speech.

669. *That fancy can beget on youthful thoughts*, which imagination combined with youth can produce.

670. *returns. I.e.*, revives in spring.

672. *cordial*, reviving the spirits, invigorating

672. *julep:* a sweet drink, especially medicinal.

673. *his*, its.

673. *crystal bounds:* the goblet in which it is contained.

675. *Nepenthes* = 'assuaging grief.' Telemachus, son of Ulysses, set out to find his father, who had not yet returned from the Trojan war. On the way he stayed at Sparta with Menelaus and Helen. To allay his grief for his father and for the death of Agamemnon, Helen put the drug nepenthes into the wine. This had been given to her by the wife of the Egyptian king Thone, and had the power of causing complete forgetfulness of all sorrow.

682. *invert the covenants of her trust*, disregard the conditions of Nature's loan.

685. *unexempt condition*, the condition from which no one is exempt.

688. *That*, 'you, who,' supplied from "you" in l. 682.

689. *wanted*, lacked.

690. Notice the vigour of the Lady's reply, expressed by the *t* sounds, the short words, and the repetition of "'twill not."

693. *the cottage*, of which Comus speaks in ll. 319–321.

694. *aspects*, appearances, (accented on the last syllable as usual at this period).

698. *visored*, masked. The visor was that part of a helmet which covered the face.

698. *forgery*, deceit.

700. *lickerish*, tempting.

701. *Were it*, even if it were.

707–708. *Stoic . . . Cynic:* two Greek schools of philosophy which agreed in scorning the pleasures of the senses.

707. *budge* was a kind of cheap fur, used especially for trimming the gowns or hoods of university professors and students. The word was then used of people who wore gowns so trimmed; there were, for instance, some men called 'budge bachelors,' who walked in the Lord Mayor's procession. "Budge doctors" would be 'professors,' so called with a touch of scorn.

707. *Stoic fur*, Stoic sect. ("Fur" follows up the idea in "budge.")

708. *Cynic tub*. Diogenes, a leading Cynic philosopher, chose to live in a tub to show his scorn of luxury or even reasonable comfort.

714. *But*, except, refers back to "wherefore."

714. *curious*, critical.

719. *hutched*, stored. 'Hutch' is still used for an antique chest. *Cf.* also 'rabbit-hutch.'

721. *pet*, fit.

722. *frieze:* a coarse woollen material.

728. *surcharged*, over-loaded.

729. *strangled*, suffocated.

732. *o'erfraught*, over-crowded.

732–736. The accumulation of precious stones in the depths

of the earth would, if not mined, give out so much light
that the inhabitants of the underworld would at last dare
to come forth in daylight, instead of only at night, as they
should.

732. *unsought diamonds.* Gems were supposed to 'grow' in the
earth, and the idea here is that if not dug out they would
increase too much.

733. *the deep.* This is sometimes taken to mean the sea. But it
more probably means the depths of the earth, where indeed one
would expect diamonds to be found rather than in the sea. It
has this meaning in *Paradise Lost* (VI, 482), and in his manuscript Milton originally wrote: "would so bestud the centre
with their starlight" (where "centre" evidently means the
centre of the earth, as in l. 382).

737. *cozened,* deluded.

742. *Unsavoury,* tasteless, insipid.

745. *brag* means (1) a boast, (2) a thing to boast of, or source of
pride.

748. *homely features. Cf.* "Home-keeping youths have ever
homely wits." Shakespeare, *The Two Gentlemen of Verona*
(I, i, 2).

750. *sorry,* poor.

750. *grain,* colour. Cf. *Il Penseroso* (33).

750–751. *ply The sampler,* work at embroidery. The phrase
'to ply the needle' is usual; this is an extension of it.

751. *tease,* comb. Wool is made fluffy by the use of a 'teazle.'

752. *vermeil-tinctured,* crimson-coloured.

755. By the double ending of the line Milton intends to
express a lack of finality, as if Comus were looking at the
Lady intently and awaiting her answer.

759. *Obtruding,* putting forward.

759. *pranked,* dressed up.

760. *bolt.* To 'bolt' flour is to sift it from the bran. The
meaning here seems to be that Vice separates one lot of
arguments from another, and uses those that happen to suit
her purpose.

762–763. *do not charge . . . As if she would,* do not accuse Nature
of wishing that . . .

767. *spare Temperance.* Answering Comus's ridicule in "a pet of temperance" (721).

768. *I.e.,* if every poor man had his fair share of the excess which a pampered few enjoy the bounty of Nature would be justly and equally divided, and nothing left over or wasted.

774. Answering what Comus said in l. 728 ff.

774. *store,* abundance.

775. Answering what Comus said in l. 723.

780. Answering what Comus said in l. 737.

785. *mystery:* doctrine learnt by divine revelation.

788. *thou art worthy.* I.e., you are not worthy to know.

790. *dear.* I.e., to Comus himself.

792. *convinced,* refuted.

793. *uncontrollèd,* uncontrollable. See note on *L'Allegro* (40).

794. *rapt,* transported. See note on *Il Penseroso* (40).

797. *the brute Earth,* unreasoning (although without the power of reasoning). A translation of Horace's *bruta tellus.*

797. *nerves,* sinews, as in l. 660. Here meaning 'strength.'

798. *thy magic structures:* the "stately palace" indicated in the stage directions before l. 659.

800–806. This is, of course, an 'aside.'

800. *She fables not,* does not speak falsely.

800. *I do fear.* Comus realizes that the Lady is supported by some divine power, of which he is afraid although he too is immortal.

803. *the wrath of Jove.* I.e., 'wrathful Jove,' a Latin turn of speech.

804. *Speaks.* Used in a double sense, (1) speaks thunder, 'utters thunder'; (2) speaks the chains of Erebus, 'pronounces sentence of imprisonment in Erebus.'

804. *Erebus:* a gloomy place under the earth, on the way down to Hades.

805. *Saturn's crew.* Zeus (Jove) waged war against his father Kronos (Saturn), son of Uranus and Ge (Heaven and Earth), Kronos being helped by his brothers and sisters the Titans. In the end Zeus won, and the Titans were cast down under the earth.

808. *canon laws:* strictly, laws of the church, applied by Comus ironically to the laws of his own unholy rule.

808. *foundation:* a monastery or similar institution.

809–810. *lees And settlings:* the solids remaining in newly made wine, which settle at the bottom and are strained off. *Cf.* "settled to itself" (595).

810. *melancholy blood.* According to the accepted theory the physical life of a man depended on four 'humours'—the melancholy, the phlegmatic, the sanguine, and the choleric. These provided the necessary moisture passing through the veins. Each 'humour' had its special qualities, affecting the mind of a man as well as his body. If the humours were equally mixed they produced perfect health of mind and body. But usually one or other predominated, causing the character to develop in a corresponding way. If this preponderance was only slight it would not matter, but if one humour greatly outweighed the others serious results would follow, both of mind and body.

The 'melancholy' which is described in *Il Penseroso* is of this slight kind, resulting only in a certain gravity of mind. The "melancholy blood" here mentioned is a more serious matter, but chiefly physical. The 'melancholy' of *L'Allegro* is of the same kind as that of *Il Penseroso*, but carried to excess. The last phase of melancholy is disease of mind and body, bringing about madness.

815. *ye should have snatched his wand.* As he had told them to do (653). They had carried out his order to break Comus's glass.

816. *rod reversed.* The regular practice in stories of magic. Circe undid her spells in this way according to Ovid, *Metamorphoses* (XIV, 300).

817. *backward mutters,* spells repeated backwards.

817. *dissevering power,* power to undo the charm.

820. If the brothers had been more careful to obey the Spirit's instructions the play would have ended with the speedy release of the Lady. But their forgetfulness makes a convenient pretext for introducing Sabrina (with appropriate theatrical devices). Sabrina being the goddess of the Severn, a

tributary of which flows past Ludlow, the episode had topical interest.

822. *Melibœus:* Spenser. He told the story of Sabrina in his *Fairy Queen* (II, x, 14–19).

823. *The soothest shepherd,* the most truthful poet.

The convention of representing poets as shepherds is the basis of all 'pastoral poetry.' Virgil in his first *Eclogue* has two shepherds, Melibœus and Tityrus. Spenser used "Tityrus" to mean Chaucer, so here Milton uses the other name for Spenser himself.

824. *a gentle Nymph.* The story of Sabrina was told by several other poets besides Spenser, and goes back to Geoffrey of Monmouth's chronicle, from which Milton himself retold it in his *History of Britain,* in prose.

The legend was that a descendant of Æneas, Brutus, conquered Albion, which was thereafter called Britain after him. After his death Corineus became king of Cornwall, and the rest of the country was divided between the three sons of Brutus. One of these, Locrine, married Corineus's daughter Gwendolen, but later deserted her and took Estrildis as his queen. They had a daughter, Sabra. But Gwendolen returned with an army and defeated Locrine. She killed him, and threw Estrildis and Sabra into a river, which was thenceforth called Sabrina or Severn, after Sabra.

For the present purpose Milton has considerably altered the background of the story.

825. *curb,* bit, as if the river were a horse, as in l. 887, "bridle in thy headlong wave."

825. *sways,* controls.

833. *The water nymphs:* the fifty Nereids, daughters of the sea-god Nereus. He was usually represented as an old man. *Cf.* l. 871, "hoary Nereus." The Nereids were friendly to mortals, so Spenser makes them carry a wounded man down to their home under the water and nurse him there, Spenser, *Fairy Queen* (III, iv, 40).

836. *reared,* raised.

836. *lank,* languid, drooping.

838. *nectared.* In the passage quoted above Spenser says that

nectar is "Good both for earthly medicine and for heavenly food."

838. *lavers:* large bowls for water.

838. *asphodel:* a plant which grew in Elysium, where the souls of heroes dwelt. It was a symbol of immortality. It is a kind of lily, and grows wild in countries bordering on the Mediterranean sea.

839. *the porch and inlet of each sense.* Cf. "the porches of mine ears," Shakespeare, *Hamlet* (I, v, 63).

840. *ambrosial,* making immortal.

841. *immortal change:* change to immortality.

845. *Helping,* curing.

845. *urchin:* hedgehog. Owing to its odd appearance and nocturnal habits it was believed to be harmful and to have magical properties. Malicious fairies and elves could take its shape.

The word still exists in 'sea-urchins,' which are prickly like hedgehogs. Small boys are called 'urchins' because they are 'imps' (elves).

845. *blast,* damage. Cf. "mildew blast" (640).

845. *ill-luck signs,* signs or omens portending ill luck.

846. *shrewd,* spiteful.

852. *the old swain:* Melibœus.

Song. Sung by the Attendant Spirit (Henry Lawes, the musician).

863. *amber-dropping.* Amber or ambergris was a kind of perfume (not the amber used for jewellery). Sabrina's hair is dressed like that of Comus's followers. Cf. ll. 105–106).

864. *honour,* chastity.

866. We now come to a long list of classical divinities, nearly all of whom have their 'stock epithets.' They are all deities of water, hence appropriately appealed to in a prayer addressed to the river-nymph Sabrina.

868. *Oceanus.* Ocean was the great stream which the Greeks believed to encircle the earth. It was personified as Oceanus (called "great" by classical poets). His wife was Tethys.

869. *Neptune:* god of the sea. Homer calls Poseidon (Neptune) "the Earth-shaker." His "mace," or sceptre, was a trident, or three-pronged spear. See notes on ll. 20 and 27.

871. *Nereus.* See note on l. 833.

872. *the Carpathian wizard:* Proteus, the 'Old Man of the Sea.' He lived in a cave on the island of Carpathus in the Mediterranean Sea, and has a "hook" (*i.e.*, a shepherd's crook) because he is the herdsman of the seals belonging to Neptune. He is called "wizard"—meaning 'wise man,' not 'magician' —like the wizards in the *Nativity Ode* (23) because he had the power of prophecy.

873. *Triton:* son of Neptune, a sea-god represented with a fish's tail, and blowing a horn made of a large shell. He acts as herald to Neptune. He is "scaly" like other sea deities.

873. *winding*, because of the winding passages inside a shell. But 'to wind a horn' means to blow it, and the phrase 'winding horn' also exists. So here we may be meant to think of Triton using the shell as a trumpet.

874. *Glaucus:* originally a mortal who became immortal by eating a certain herb. He had prophetic powers, and lived at the bottom of the sea.

875. *Leucothea* was also a mortal, called Ino. She fled from her husband, carrying with her her son Melicertes, and leapt into the sea, where she became divine and was renamed Leucothea ('the White Goddess'). Melicertes also became immortal, and was called Palæmon. The Romans called him Portumnus ('god of ports').

Glaucus, Leucothea, and Palæmon were like Sabrina in having acquired immortailty by leaping into sea or river.

877. *Thetis:* one of Nereus's daughters, and mother of Achilles. Homer calls her "silver-footed," which Milton recalls by "tinsel-slippered." "Tinsel" was a material interwoven or shot with metallic threads, or sparkles.

878. *Sirens.* See note on l. 253.

879. *Parthenope:* one of the sirens, whose tomb could be seen at Naples, which was also called Parthenope after her.

880. *Ligea:* another of the sirens. A golden comb suggests a mermaid rather than a classical siren.

894. *turkis*, turquoise.

895. *strays.* Plural.

The rippling colours of the water are 'set' as jewels in her chariot.

897. *printless*, leaving no footprint, like the elves in Shakespeare's *Tempest* (V, i, 34), "with printless foot."

907. *unblest*, accursed.

913. *cure*, remedy.

921. *Amphitrite:* a sea-goddess, wife of Neptune.

923. *Anchises:* father of Æneas, and so ancestor of Locrine. See note on l. 824.

924–931 give a picture of the real Severn, filled by streams from the Welsh hills,

> . . . petty rills
> That tumble down the snowy hills;

and liable to have its usually clear water filled with mud at times of flood:

> Nor wet October's torrent flood
> Thy molten crystal fill with mud.

In ll. 932–937 Milton changes from a natural to a very imaginative description.

928. *singed*, burning hot.

931. *molten crystal*. Describing the previously clear water.

934–937. The grammatical sequence is rather difficult to follow. Either the meaning is 'may you be crowned upon your banks with groves,' or there are two kinds of crown; (1) towers and terraces, and (2) groves of myrrh and cinnamon growing upon the banks.

934. *thy lofty head*. The river is once again personified as a maiden.

935. *many a tower and terrace*, such as Ludlow castle itself. For the idea of a crown of towers *cf.* Cybele's crown, *Arcades* (21).

946–955. A picture of what was actually happening.

949. *gratulate*, welcome.

957. A longer line, to end this episode.

958–959. Cf. *L'Allegro* (97–98).

960. *without duck or nod*. The clumsy curtseys and countrified dances of the shepherds must now make way for more courtly and elegant dances.

963. *Mercury:* the messenger of the gods. He often leads the dances of the nymphs in Greek art and poetry.

964. *mincing*, stepping daintily.

964. *Dryades:* wood-nymphs.

965. *leas,* meadows.

966 *ff.* Addressed to the persons in whose honour the masque was performed, as was done in *Arcades.*

970. *timely,* early.

972. *assays,* trials.

976–983. The likeness of this passage to Ariel's song in *The Tempest* is obvious, and the Spirit here has much in common with Ariel, and also with Puck in *A Midsummer Night's Dream.*

976. The Spirit now returns to the heavenly region from which he came.

977. *climes.* Lands. Cf. *Arcades* (24).

978. *Where day never shuts his eye,* where the sun never sets. The sun is often called the 'eye of day.'

982. *Hesperus and his daughters three.* See note on l. 393.

984. *crispèd* probably means 'ruffled by the wind,' like the "crisped brooks" in *Paradise Lost* (IV, 237).

985. *spruce,* dainty.

986. *Graces:* three goddesses, who personify charm, beauty, and joy. See note on *L'Allegro* (15).

986. *Hours:* goddesses personifying the seasons, especially spring and summer. They are often joined with the Graces in classical art and poetry.

989. *west winds:* Zephyrs, often mentioned in poetry as bringing warmth and sweet scents.

989. *musky,* scented.

990. *cedarn alleys,* avenues of cedars.

991. *Nard* (spikenard) and cassia are sweet-scented spices.

992. *Iris:* the goddess of the rainbow. *Cf.* l. 83.

993. *blow,* cause to bloom.

995. *purfled,* embroidered.

995. *shew.* For the rhyme *cf.* ll. 511, 512, and note.

996. *Elysian,* heavenly. See note on *L'Allegro* (147).

997. *if your ears be true. I.e.,* 'if your minds can understand the hidden meaning,' unlike Comus, who could not do so—see ll. 784–787.

What exactly this hidden meaning or allegory is has been

much discussed, but none of the explanations seems completely satisfactory.

999. *Adonis.* See note on *Nativity Ode* (204).

1002. *the Assyrian queen:* Aphrodite, or Ashtaroth as she was called in Syria, where her worship originated.

The story of Adonis is related by Spenser, *Fairy Queen* (III, 6), with much allegorical elaboration; Milton was no doubt influenced by this, as he knew Spenser's work well and greatly admired it. Spenser also mentions Cupid and Psyche in the same place.

1003. *sheen,* brightness.

1004. *Cupid,* the son of Aphrodite, loved Psyche ('the soul'), but their marriage was prevented by Aphrodite. Psyche endured many trials and afflictions, but in the end the gods permitted the marriage, and Psyche was given immortality.

1004. *advanced,* raised (to heaven)—explaining "celestial."

1011. *Youth and Joy.* Milton's version of 'Pleasure,' who was the child of Cupid and Psyche according to the legend.

1012–1017. The verse again reminds us of Ariel's song.

1015. *bowed,* curved.

1015. *welkin,* sky.

1015. *slow,* gradually.

1017. *the corners of the moon,* the 'horns' of the moon. *Cf.* Shakespeare, *Macbeth* (III, v, 23–24).

> Upon the corner of the moon
> There hangs a vapourous drop profound.

1021. *the sphery chime:* the music of the spheres. (See Appendix.)

1023. *Heaven itself would stoop to her.* If virtue by herself is not quite strong enough Heaven will help her. The Elder Brother expressed this idea in ll. 453 *ff.*

1018–1024. These lines sum up the general purport of *Comus,* and serve as parting words to the audience. Although Chastity is the subject of the central scene (the argument between Comus and the Lady), the theme is widened to include virtue in general in the Attendant Spirit's song (966–975) when he presents the three young people to their parents. This wider theme is suited to its place here, where it is addressed to the audience in general.

Lycidas

See Introduction, Section V.

Edward King, the "Lycidas" of the poem, was, like Milton, a student at Christ's College. He was, however, some years younger, and there is no evidence that he was an intimate friend of Milton's, though they must have known each other. He was evidently a good scholar and something of a poet, and was much liked by his contemporaries. On a journey to Ireland in August 1637 he lost his life in a shipwreck.

Some of King's friends arranged to publish a book of poems in his honour, a thing fairly often done; Milton was asked to contribute, and wrote *Lycidas* for this purpose.

The name "Lycidas" is given to a shepherd in the pastoral poems of Theocritus and Virgil.

1–5. These lines refer to Milton's resolution to devote himself entirely to study, in order to prepare himself fully for his great vocation of poet, and to write no more poetry till it should be completed. But he felt bound to comply with the request to write an elegy for Edward King. He had similarly written during this time *Arcades* and *Comus*, also at particular requests.

1–2. *laurels . . . myrtles . . . ivy.* These were used for the crowns of poets. By plucking their berries Milton means writing poetry.

2. *brown*, dark in colour. Cf. *Il Penseroso* (134).

2. *never sere*, evergreen.

3. *crude*, unripe, because Milton still thought that he lacked "inward ripeness," as he wrote in the sonnet *On His being arrived at the Age of Twenty-three.*

4. *rude*, unskilful.

5. *mellowing year:* the season which should have ripened them.

192

6. *constraint*, compulsion.

6. *occasion*, necessity.

6. *dear* is used, as often at this time, of anything that affects one intimately, whether welcome or unpleasant. So "my dearest foe," Shakespeare, *Hamlet* (I, ii, 182).

7. *Compel*. In the singular because "constraint" and "occasion" are really one subject.

9. *peer*, equal.

10. An echo of Virgil, *Eclogues* (X, 3).

10–11. *He knew . . . to sing*. A Latin form of speech, meaning "he knew how to sing." Cf. *Comus* (87). King seems to have had a considerable reputation as a poet among his contemporaries at Cambridge, though none of his poetry, except a few Latin verses, is known.

11. *rhyme*, verse.

13. *welter*, toss up and down. Cf. *Nativity Ode* (124).

14. *melodious tear*, poetical lament. Elegies were often referred to as 'tears.'

15. *Begin*. This formula takes us back to the Greek and Roman pastoral poems, which often start with an invocation of this sort.

15. *Sisters of the sacred well*: the Muses. See note on *Il Penseroso* (47).

19–22. The meaning is, 'As I am writing an elegy for Lycidas, so may some other poet write one for me when I come to die.'

19. *So. Sc.* 'as I write an elegy for Lycidas.'

19. *Muse* here means a poet.

20. *lucky words*: words which in themselves bear a good sense, like 'farewell' ('fare well'). Also perhaps 'felicitous' in the sense of 'appropriate.'

20. *urn*, tomb, or grave.

21. *he*, masculine, though referring to the "Muse," since an actual poet is really meant.

23. *For* gives the reason why Milton expects the same honour to be paid to him as to Edward King.

25–36. In the form of pastoral convention, these lines refer to the life of students at Cambridge which Milton and King had in common, though we need not try to explain every

N

phrase by reference to actual persons or activities; most of them belong to the tradition of the pastoral.

25. *high lawns*, grassy hills. Cf. *Nativity Ode* (85).

27. *drove*. *Sc.* our flocks.

28. *What time the gray-fly*. *I.e.*, 'the gray-fly, when . . .' The gray-fly must be some kind of gnat.

28. *winds*, blows.

28. *sultry*, because it is heard in the hottest time of the day.

29. *Battening*, feeding, fattening.

30. *the star*. "The star that bids the shepherd fold." *Comus* (93).

32. *ditties*, songs.

33. *Tempered*, attuned to, accompanied on.

33. *the oaten flute*. See note on *Comus* (345).

34. *Satyrs . . . Fauns*: pastoral divinities, represented with the horns and hoofs of goats ("cloven heel").

36. *Damætas*: another classical shepherd's name. It may refer to some person of Milton's Cambridge days.

38. *must*, are destined. Cf. *Nativity Ode* (150 and 153).

40. *gadding*, straggling, wayward.

41. *their echoes*. *I.e.*, the echoes which had their homes in the caves, like Echo in *Comus* (230–231) (where see note).

44. *Fanning*, moving like fans. In Virgil's *Sixth Eclogue* the oaks move their topmost boughs when Silenus sings. Most of the ideas in these lines (39–44) come from Greek or Latin originals.

46. *taint-worm* was obviously dangerous to cattle, but we cannot be sure exactly what creature is meant.

46. *weanling*, lately weaned, young.

47. *wardrope*. So pronounced in Milton's day; we now say 'wardrobe.'

48. *blows*, blooms. In *Comus* (993) it is transitive, 'cause to bloom.'

50–55. Here again Milton goes back to classical models. Theocritus made an appeal to the nymphs (which Milton closely follows), and Virgil to the naiads.

52. *steep*: probably a mountain in Denbighshire (Wales), which was reputed to be the burying-place of the Druids.

53. *bards*: poets, especially the ancient Celtic minstrels.

53. *Druids:* here appropriately mentioned because besides their other functions they were also poets. Milton speaks of them with interest in his *History of Britain* and elsewhere.

54. *Mona:* Anglesey. It was once well-wooded ("shaggy"), but is now bare. It was the chief centre of the Druids.

55. *Deva:* Dee.

55. *wizard*, sacred, or magical. *Cf.* "ancient hallowed Dee," Milton, *Vacation Exercise* (98). The Dee formed the boundary between England and Wales, and was regarded as sacred, many legends and beliefs being attached to it, the best known being that by changes in its course it foretold the fortunes of England and of Wales. It is 'wizard' in the same sense as Proteus is, *Comus* (872), as foretelling the future.

All the places mentioned are within sight of the place where the shipwreck took place. King had sailed from Chester (on the Dee). The interest Milton took in the ancient history and legends of Britain finds appropriate expression here.

56. *fondly.* foolishly. *Cf.* sonnet *On his blindness* (8).

57. *for* explains "fondly." It is useless to think of what might have happened if the nymphs had been at hand, for they could not have helped.

58. *could.* *Sc.* 'do.'

58. *the Muse*, Calliope, the goddess of song.

58, *Orpheus.* See note on *L'Allegro* (145). He met his death at the hands of the Thracian mænads (women who worshipped the god Dionysus in wild ecstasies on the mountains). They cut off his head, and threw it into the river Hebrus, whence it drifted across the sea to the island of Lesbos. Milton mentions the legend again in *Paradise Lost* (VII, 32–39), with a reference to himself.

59. *enchanting*, literally, because by his music Orpheus could draw beasts and even trees to himself as by a spell.

61. *rout.* A noisy, disorderly crowd, like the monsters who followed Comus.

The point of these lines is that the Muse Calliope was a much more powerful divinity than the nymphs, yet could not rescue her own son, Orpheus, himself a much greater poet than Lycidas.

64–84. In these lines Milton speaks of the labour involved in the profession of poet, of the glory that may be won, and of the risks that attend it, all under the guise and in the terms of pastoral poetry. He is thinking of the highest kind of poetry, for which he strongly believed that the poet must prepare himself by severe self-discipline and thorough and profound study. (This is the meaning of "uncessant care" and "strictly meditate.")

64. *boots*, avails.

64. *uncessant*, incessant. *Cf.* "unsufferable," *Nativity Ode* (8).

65. *shepherd's trade*. *I.e.*, poetry.

66. *meditate the Muse*. See note on *Comus* (547).

66. *thankless*, either because "the Muse" cannot save the poet from death or because poetry does not bring any material profit.

67. *others:* contemporary poets who wrote on less serious subjects. Or merely light-hearted people in general, who enjoy themselves without much thought.

67. *use*, are accustomed. We still find this meaning in the past tense ('used to'), but no longer in the present tense.

68. *Amaryllis . . . Neæra*. Names of shepherdesses going back to classical originals.

70. *Fame is the spur*. In the *Seventh Prolusion* Milton gives the opposite view—"but yet to have no thought of glory when we do well is above all glory."

70. *clear*, pure. Cf. *Comus* (381), "He that has light within his own clear breast."

71. *That last infirmity of noble mind*. The Roman historian Tacitus seems to have been the first to say this, but many writers have expressed the idea since. Milton's version has become proverbial (though usually wrongly quoted). There are surprisingly few such 'quotations' from Milton.

75. *the blind Fury:* Atropos. See note on *Arcades* (63–73). She is really one of the Fates, not a Fury, but Milton calls her a Fury in his indignation.

75. *blind*, probably because Fortune is represented as blind, and the "Fury" here is equivalent to Fortune. She does not see what she is doing.

76. *slits*, cuts.

76. "*But not the praise.*" Some verb must be supplied from "slits." Verity points out that its omission suggests the quickness of Phœbus's reply.

77. *Phœbus:* Apollo, god of poets.

77. *touched my trembling ears.* Virgil, *Eclogues* (VI, 3), says that Apollo pulled his ear to stop him from going too fast.

79. *Nor* depends on "lies."

79. *foil:* a thin sheet of metal put behind a gem to show it up (*cf.* 'tin-foil'). Here, of course, not literal, but meaning any bright setting.

80. *broad rumour,* widespread fame.

81. *by those pure eyes,* through the clear sight and fair judgment of Jove.

81–83. Another instance of a Christian idea expressed in pagan terms—"Jove" = God.

83. *lastly,* finally.

85. *Arethuse* (Arethusa). See note on *Arcades* (30). The mention of Arethusa reminds us of the pastoral poems of Theocritus, who was a Sicilian, and mentions the fountain of Arethusa in his first *Idyll.*

86. *Mincius:* a river flowing into the Po near Mantua, the birthplace of Virgil, who describes it in his *Eclogues* and *Georgics.* It is "honoured" by being mentioned in this way.

　　The mention of Arethusa and Mincius marks Milton's return to the pastoral style after the words spoken by Phœbus.

86. *vocal reeds.* Reeds are "vocal" because they can be made into shepherds' pipes.

87. *That strain:* Phœbus's words.

88. *my oat.* I.e., my verse in pastoral style. See note on *Comus* (345).

89. *the herald of the sea,* Triton. See note on *Comus* (873).

90. *plea,* defence. He could have been accused of causing or at least permitting King's death, since the sea was his domain.

91. *felon,* cruel.

93. *gust of rugged wings,* gust with rugged wings.

93. *rugged,* rough. See note on *L'Allegro* (9).

94. *beakèd,* projecting like a bird's beak.

96. *Hippotades:* Æolus, son of Hippotes; he was made ruler over the winds, which he kept imprisoned in a cave.

97. *I.e.*, not a single wind had got out of the cave.

98. *level*, smooth, but also perhaps giving an idea of the extent of open sea. *Cf.* "the flat sea," *Comus* (375).

99. *Panope.* One of the fifty daughters of Nereus, who might be expected to befriend sailors. See note on *Comus* (833).

101. *Built in the eclipse*, a proverbially unlucky time.

103. *Camus.* The river-god of the Cam, here standing for the University of Cambridge.

103. *footing slow*, the Cam being a sluggish stream.

104. *bonnet:* a man's hat. The hats worn by Doctors at Cambridge are still called 'bonnets.'

105. *figures dim:* probably symbolical figures embroidered on the cloak or bonnet of Camus. It has also been suggested that they are streaks or spots which appear on the leaves of sedge as it withers.

106. *sanguine flower:* the hyacinth, which was said to have sprung from the blood of a youth called Hyacinthus, whom Apollo accidentally killed at a game of quoit-throwing. ('Sanguine' means 'bloody,' or 'blood-red.') In his grief Apollo caused the flower to be marked with the letters *aiai*, which spell the Greek exclamation for woe, and which it is still supposed to bear—"inscribed with woe."

107. *pledge*, child.

109. *The Pilot of the Galilean lake:* St Peter. Christ stood in his boat when preaching to the crowd beside the Sea of Galilee, St Luke (v, 3).

110. *Two massy keys:* the keys of the Kingdom of Heaven promised to him by Christ, St Matthew (xvi, 19). According to church tradition there are two keys, but the idea that they are of different metals and serve different purposes is Milton's.

111. *The golden . . . the iron.* So in *Paradise Lost* (II, 327) God rules over heaven with a golden sceptre, and over hell with an iron one.

111. *amain*, with force.

112. *mitred*, wearing the bishop's mitre, as being the first bishop.

112. *bespake.* See note on *Nativity Ode* (76).

113. Edward King was to have been a clergyman.

113–131. The basis of this passage is the parable in St John (x, 1), "He that entereth not by the door into the sheepfold, but climbeth up some other way, the same is a thief and a robber." Later, in his prose works, Milton continued the attack, and numerous parallels are to be found throughout his writings, both verse and prose.

114. *Cf.* sonnet *To the Lord General Cromwell* (14).

116. *care,* duty.

116. *little reckoning made.* Cf. *Comus* (642).

117. *the shearers' feast* was a rural festival as well known as the harvest-home. Here it stands for the good posts the corrupt clergy hope to get.

119. *Blind mouths!* Milton's indignation is concentrated in this startling pair of words. "Mouths," in addition, bears two possible meanings at the same time; (1) gluttons (of course in a metaphorical sense, 'greedy for money'), (2) low forms of life which do little beyond feeding.

The blindness is, of course, spiritual blindness.

119–121. Milton now attacks the ignorance of the clergy, which he often did later.

120. *sheep-hook:* the pastoral staff, representing the duties of the clergy.

122. *are sped,* have succeeded.

123. *when they list.* I.e., they only preach when they wish to.

123. *lean,* dry, and giving no nourishment.

123. *flashy,* tasteless, insipid. A different word from 'flashy' in the ordinary sense.

123. *songs:* their sermons.

124. *scrannel,* thin. The word is known only in dialects of the North of England.

124. *pipes.* The shepherd's pipe again, of course in a metaphorical sense. Notice how the sound of this line suggests the harshness of the pipe's sound.

126. *rank mist.* I.e., poisonous doctrine.

126. *draw,* breathe in.

128. *the grim wolf:* the Roman Church.

129. *and nothing said.* *I.e.*, without opposition. Archbishop
Laud, the King and Queen, and others were suspected of
secretly favouring the revival of the Roman Catholic Church.

130. *that two-handed engine.* It is impossible to discuss the
numerous explanations of this phrase which have been put
forward. Many of them can be dismissed at once as referring
to events which only occurred after it was written. The only
point to be considered is what a contemporary reader could
have been expected to make of it; and this could hardly have
been anything but simply though vaguely the vengeance of
God ("the sword of the Lord"). Milton was not concerned
with an exact prophecy, but with a threat of some terrible
but vague catastrophe—a much more terrifying matter.

An *engine* is any instrument or tool, especially a weapon.
We still occasionally hear of 'engines of war.'

130. *two-handed*, wielded by both hands. Here the "engine"
is one of the huge swords in use in the sixteenth and seventeenth centuries, and often mentioned—*e.g.*, Shakespeare,
2 Henry VI (II, i, 45), "Come with thy two-hand sword."

130. *at the door.* *I.e.*, of the sheepfold (the Church) into which
the corrupt clergy had crept and intruded and climbed.

131. A single blow would be enough.

132. *Return, Alpheus.* A sudden change of mood, reverting
to the gentle, pastoral style after the "dread Voice" of the
preceding fierce passage. The transition is like that at l. 85,
which has in a way prepared us for it, but the present one is
more startling.

Alpheus here corresponds to Arethusa (85), and like her
is invoked as representing pastoral poetry, since his stream
joined hers in Sicily.

On Alpheus see note on *Arcades* (30).

133. *shrunk thy stream.* *I.e.*, checked the flow of the pastoral
verse.

133. *Sicilian*, pastoral. See note on l. 85.

136. *use*, dwell.

137. *wanton*, changeable. "The wind bloweth where it listeth."
St John (iii, 8).

138. *whose.* *I.e.*, of the valleys.

l. 138. *the swart star:* Sirius, the Dog-star.

138. *swart* means dark, or brown, here probably describing the effect on vegetation of the heat of the star, which appears at the hottest part of the summer, the 'dog days.'

138. *sparely,* seldom.

138. *looks,* casts a baleful glance, the opposite of the stars in the *Nativity Ode* (70), which "Stand fixed in steadfast gaze," and like the "dire-looking planet" in *Arcades* (52). On the 'influence' of the stars shed by their gaze see note on *Nativity Ode* (71).

139. *quaint,* dainty, or fanciful.

139. *enamelled.* See note on *Arcades* (84).

139. *eyes,* flowers.

141. *purple,* make purple. In Milton, as in the classical poets, 'purple' means a rich glowing colour, not precisely 'red,' so that here the word really means 'make brilliant.'

142. *rathe,* early.

142. *forsaken,* probably means 'unmarried,' which in fact Milton originally wrote, perhaps thinking of

> . . . pale primroses
> That die unmarried.
> (Shakespeare, *Winter's Tale*, IV, iii, 122).

The primrose is forsaken, or unmarried, because it grows in the shade, where the sun cannot reach it. The sun is often spoken of as the lover of the flowers.

143. *crow-toe:* identified with the hyacinth in old 'herbals,' or botanical books.

144. *freaked,* spotted.

146. *well-attired.* Cf. "Solomon in all his glory was not arrayed like one of these," St Matthew (vi, 29).

146. *woodbine:* either honeysuckle or convolvulus.

149. *amaranthus:* actually the flower also called 'love-lies-bleeding,' but in Milton's mind it is rather the mythical flower which was supposed never to fade (the literal meaning of the word 'amaranthus'), and which was therefore a symbol of immortality.

151. *laureate,* crowned with laurel, referring to *Lycidas* and

the other poems in the volume dedicated to the memory of
Edward King.

152. 'To assuage our grief a little, let us allow ourselves to
play with a fanciful idea'—*i.e.*, that Lycidas's body is lying on
a flower-decked bier instead of being tossed on the sea as it
really is. This last consideration is the point of the following
lines (154–164).

154. *shores*, shallow waters, as contrasted with "sounding
seas." *Cf.* note on *Il Penseroso* (74).

157. *whelming*, overwhelming in the literal sense of engulfing.

158. *monstrous world*, world of monsters. *Cf.* "monstrous
rout," *Comus* (533).

159. *moist vows*. Vows (prayers) to the god of the sea, or else
'tearful prayers.'

For this use of "vows" cf. *Arcades* (6).

160. *the fable of Bellerus*, the scene of the legend of Bellerus.
The old name for Cornwall was Bellerium, from which
Milton appears to have invented Bellerus. He originally
wrote "Corineus."

161. *the great vision:* the archangel Michael. He was said to
have appeared seated on a stone seat looking out to sea, on
St Michael's Mount (so called after him) on the coast of
Cornwall. The seat, known as 'St Michael's Chair,' is still to
be seen.

A monastery was later built on the Mount, and finally a
fortress; hence "the guarded mount."

162. *Namancos and Bayona's hold*. These places are on the
north-west coast of Spain, toward which St Michael's
Mount faces. Namancos is a district adjoining Cape Finisterre
in Spain (which corresponds in both name and situation to
Land's End). Bayona lies further south.

It was an old literary tradition that St Michael's Mount
looked directly toward Spain, keeping guard as it were
against the enemy there, a tradition which probably dates
from the time of the Armada.

The names of Namancos and Bayona caused considerable
difficulty for a long time, as it was not known to what they
referred, Namancos not being shown in most maps, and

Bayona being supposed to be Bayonne in France. It is now established that in Mercator's atlas, published shortly before *Lycidas* was written, both appeared in the map of Galicia (though not in that of Spain as a whole). Milton must have been struck by the sound of the two names, and has used them instead of 'Spain' or some equivalent, so making this geographical detail both exciting and poetical.

163. *Look homeward Angel now.* The Angel is St Michael, who is exhorted to turn away from Spain and look instead at the coast of England, where he will see and grieve for the dead Lycidas.

Some people think that "Angel now" means Lycidas himself, now an angel in heaven; but this does not fit in well with what follows. And "Looks toward Namancos" evidently balances "Look homeward now," both referring to St Michael.

164. *ye dolphins.* A Greek story relates how the poet Arion, having been captured by pirates, escaped by the help of a dolphin. He stood on deck and sang, which attracted a dolphin, and jumping on to its back he was carried safely to land.

Dolphins are, according to Burton's *Anatomy*, "as common experience evinceth, much affected by music," so that it would be natural that one should rescue the musical Lycidas. In fact, one of the other poems in the memorial volume suggests this:

> Why did not some officious dolphin hie
> To be his ship and pilot through the fry
> Of wondering nymphs . . .?

164. *waft*, often used of carrying over water.

165. *Weep no more, woeful shepherds, weep no more.* Recalling the first line of the poem, "Yet once more, O ye laurels, and once more."

166. *your sorrow. I.e.*, 'the object of your sorrow.'

168. *day-star:* the sun.

170. *tricks*, dresses, decks. Cf. *Il Penseroso* (123).

173. *Him that walked the waves:* Christ. See St Matthew (xiv, 25).

174. *other.* *Sc.* than those on earth.

175. *nectar:* any fragrant liquid. Cf. *Comus* (838).

175. *oozy,* wet with sea-water.

176. *unexpressive,* inexpressible. Cf. *Nativity Ode* (116).

176. *nuptial song.* At the "marriage of the Lamb," Revelation (xix, 7).

181. Referring to Revelation xxi, 4. "And God shall wipe away all tears from their eyes."

183. *Genius.* See note on *Nativity Ode* (186). Here again we find the mixture of classical and Christian ideas.

184. *thy large recompense,* the ample recompense made to you.

184. *good,* propitious.

186. *uncouth,* unknown, and probably 'unskilled' also. Milton is here speaking of himself.

188. *tender,* delicate, or light to the touch.

188. *stops.* See note on *Comus* (345).

188. *various,* varied, alluding to the changes of feeling.

188. *quills:* the hollow reeds forming the Pan's-pipes.

189. *Doric.* The Doric dialect of Greek was spoken in Sicily, and was used by the Greek pastoral poets. Theocritus and Moschus, who were Sicilians, each wrote an elegy on the death of a friend.

190. *stretched out all the hills.* *I.e.,* made long shadows of the hills.

192. *twitched,* pulled on. Putting on his cloak suggests making a sudden decision.

193. *To-morrow to fresh woods.* This line is sometimes said to refer to Milton's plans for a journey to Italy, which he may have already formed. Or it may mark his decision to write no more pastoral poetry, Or, again, it may merely be his farewell to this particular poem.

This is one more of the few 'familiar quotations' from Milton, though it is usually misquoted, with 'fields' instead of "woods."

The last eight lines make a well-defined stanza, and give the impression of the poet having come to a definite decision after the uncertainties of the rest of the poem.

Sonnets

THERE are two main types of English sonnet, differing on account of their different rhyme schemes. The first is the Italian or Petrarchian type, the second the English or Shakespearean. (Petrarchian and Shakespearean are the usual terms.) In the Petrarchian type there are only two units of rhyme. The first is of eight lines, and the second of six, making fourteen in all. In other words one series of rhymes goes through, and ends with, the first set of lines, or octave; and another, different set of rhymes goes through the second set of lines, or sestett. In the Shakespearean type there are four units of rhyme, three of four lines each (or quatrains), and one couplet. There are some variations within each type of sonnet. Milton's are of the Petrarchian type, and preserve the scheme of octave and sestett; but within these he varies the order of the rhymes.

In poetry different forms condition different kinds or different arrangements of sense. The Limerick form, for instance, insists that the sense should not be solemn. In the Shakespearean form of sonnet the couplet is strongly contrasted with the three preceding quatrains, and tends to comment on them or sum them up. The quatrains themselves tend to make the same point, but with increased emphasis: sometimes in the third quatrain the poet makes a new point; sometimes the process of emphasizing the same point continues through the third quatrain. Here is a sonnet of Shakespeare, whose subject is the contrast between the mortality of worldly things and the immortality which the person addressed will enjoy through being celebrated in these verses. The first two quatrains speak with gathering emphasis of the mortality of things. The third says that the person addressed will escape this mortality. The couplet clinches these different statements by adding that this escape is through the immortality of verse.

Shall I compare thee to a summer's day?
Thou art more lovely and more temperate;
Rough winds do shake the darling buds of May,
And summer's lease hath all too short a date:
Sometime too hot the eye of heaven shines,
And often is his gold complexion dimm'd;
And every fair from fair sometime declines,
By chance or nature's changing course untrimm'd;
But thy eternal summer shall not fade
Nor lose possession of that fair thou owest,
Nor shall Death brag thou wander'st in his shade,
When in eternal lines to time thou growest:
   So long as men can breathe or eyes can see,
   So long lives this and this gives life to thee.

The Petrarchian sonnet form, being less broken metrically, encourages either a contrast between the octave and sestett or a fairly continuous flow of thought. Milton's sonnets vary between these two procedures. The sonnet beginning "Captain or Colonel . . ." makes a contrast between the two metrical units of the sonnet. The octave talks of the fame that generous deeds can give: the sestett recommends a specific generous deed. But more often than not Milton likes to continue the flow of his thought, and he does this by making the grammatical sense not, as in the above sonnet, stop at the end of the octave but flow over from the octave into the sestett, so that there is no pause of the voice at the end of the octave or first rhyme-unit. He began this practice with his earliest English sonnet "O Nightingale."

Both types of sonnet have been written since Milton's day, but Milton's example has proved far more popular than Shakespeare's.

See Introduction, Section VI.

1. TO THE NIGHTINGALE

The theme of this sonnet is an old idea that to hear the nightingale before the cuckoo was lucky for lovers, the reverse unlucky. This idea was taken up by several medieval French poets, and is also found in a poem called *The Cuckoo and the Nightingale*, which used to be attributed to Chaucer, and which Milton must have known. In it the poet goes out hoping to hear the nightingale, but hears the cuckoo first. In the end, however, the nightingale promises to be there and sing before the cuckoo next year.

This is one of Milton's earliest poems, written probably soon after the *Nativity Ode*.

4. *the jolly Hours.* For the Hours see note on *Comus* (986).

4. *jolly* may have its old meaning of 'pretty.' But Homer calls the Hours "gladsome," so it probably means 'pleasant' here. The word has deteriorated in meaning since Milton's day, as many others have.

4. *lead on.* A metaphor from the dance. Cf. *Paradise Lost* (IV, 266):

> . . . universal Pan,
> Knit with the Graces and the Hours in dance
> Led on th'eternal Spring.

5. *close the eye of day.* *I.e.*, lull day to sleep. Cf. *Comus* (978), "Where day never shuts his eye."

6. *First heard.* *I.e.*, if heard first.

6. *shallow* describes both the irresponsible habits of the cuckoo, and the poorness of its note as a song.

8. *that amorous power:* love.

9. *timely*, early.

9. *the rude bird of hate:* the cuckoo, as being unfavourable to lovers.

11. *too late:* when Milton had already heard the cuckoo.

II. ON HIS BEING ARRIVED TO THE AGE OF TWENTY-THREE

Milton's twenty-third birthday was in December 1631.

The sonnet was originally enclosed in a letter from Milton to some older friend, who had evidently spoken to Milton urging him to give up what he considered purposeless study, and take up some profession. Milton explains that the delay is not due to laziness or thoughtlessness, but to a conscientious belief in the need for thorough preparation for his true profession, speaking of "a contrary command from above, and the terrible seizing of him that hid the talent"—a reference to the parable in St Matthew (xxv, 14–30), repeated in the later sonnet on his blindness. He ends by saying "Yet that you may see that I am sometimes suspicious of myself and do take notice of a certain belatedness in myself, I am the bolder to send you some of my nightward thoughts some while since, since they come in fitly, made up in a Petrarchian stanza."

3. *career*, speed.

4. Milton overlooks the fact that he had already written the *Nativity Ode*, and probably *L'Allegro* and *Il Penseroso*, besides several smaller poems and a number of translations in verse.

4. *shew'th*. Rhyming with "truth." Cf. *Comus* (511–512, 994–996, and notes).

5. Milton apparently always looked young for his age. He himself says that he looked ten years younger than he actually was even when over forty (*Defensio Secunda*). He had a very fair complexion. These characteristics caused him to be called "The Lady of Christ's."

5. *semblance*, appearance, as contrasted with "inward ripeness" (l. 7).

8. *timely-happy*, fortunate in reaching maturity sooner.

9. *it*, "inward ripeness" (l. 7).

10. *still*, always.

10–11. *even to*, corresponding to.

13–14. These are difficult lines. They may mean (1) 'All this holds good only if I have grace to use my lot in this way, namely as if I were always in the presence of God my Master,' taking "so As ever" closely together; (2) 'My whole life is under the direct surveillance of God, provided that I have grace to recognize this in the use I make of it,' taking "All is as ever . . ." together.

III. When the Assault was intended to the City

After the battle of Edgehill (October 23, 1642) the King advanced towards London, his forces plundering every place to which they came. On November 12 he defeated a Parliamentary force at Brentford, which also was plundered. Every one expected that he would at once attack London, and the citizens prepared to defend it, calling up the 'trained bands' and digging trenches, being convinced that if the King once entered the city it would be destroyed and its inhabitants killed. However, the 'trained bands' and some forces which had escaped after the battle of Edgehill gathered at Turnham Green, and the King, finding a stronger force opposing him than he had expected, gave up his plan and retreated on November 13.

Milton was at this time living in Aldersgate Street, which was then just outside the city boundaries. It is a remarkable proof of his courage and calmness that he was able to write this sonnet at such a time, as he seems to have done. But the idea that he fastened it to his door in the hope of deterring would-be plunderers has no foundation, nor would such an act have been likely to effect its object.

1. *Colonel* was still pronounced with three syllables in Milton's day.

2. 'Whom chance may permit to seize.'

5. *charms:* magic powers of poetry.

10. *The great Emathian conqueror:* Alexander the Great. After he had conquered Greece Alexander moved northward. In his absence the city of Thebes revolted. Alexander thereupon returned, and overcame and destroyed the city (335 B.C.). The story goes that hearing that the poet Pindar had been born and lived in Thebes Alexander gave orders that his house should be spared, and even showed favour to his descendants.

Pindar was a Greek poet who lived about 500 B.C., and wrote magnificent odes in honour of the victors at the great games held at sacred festivals, among whom was one of Alexander's ancestors.

Emathia was a district of Macedonia, but the name was often used by poets to mean the whole country.

12. *repeated*, recited. The phrase "repeated air" is a Latin form of speech (*cf.* note on *Comus* (48)), and is equivalent to 'the repetition [recital] of the air.'

13. *sad Electra's poet:* Euripides, author of the play *Electra*. When the Spartans and their allies conquered Athens (404 B.C.) they at first intended to raze the city to the ground. But at a banquet a minstrel recited a chorus from the play, which so moved the assembled generals that they gave up their

intention, as being too cruel treatment for a city which had produced such great men. They did, however, destroy all the walls.

13. *sad* probably qualifies "Electra," not the "poet" as has sometimes been suggested.

IV. TO THE LADY MARGARET LEY

James Ley ("that good Earl") was created Earl of Marlborough by Charles I. He had been Lord Chief Justice, Lord High Treasurer, and Lord President of the Council. He retired in 1628, and died soon after.

Lady Margaret Ley was the elder of two daughters who were still living with him at the time of his death, so that she would naturally have been able to tell Milton much about him. She married John Hobson, of the Isle of Wight, and they were living in London when the sonnet was written (probably between 1642 and 1645), being near neighbours and intimate friends of Milton. Her father had been a royalist (though Milton implies that he did not really approve of Charles's policy), but her husband became an officer in the Parliamentary army.

4. *more in himself content*, preferring private life.

5. *the sad breaking of that Parliament*. The Parliament which began the stand against the King, and was dissolved on March 10, 1629, after scenes of turmoil. Four days later the Earl died. Milton suggests that his death was caused or hastened by the shock of this event, and may well have been told this by the Earl's daughter.

5–6. *breaking . . . broke*. A sort of pun, the same word being used in different senses. The play on words heightens the feeling of the passage. See note on *Nativity Ode* (83).

6. *dishonest*, dishonourable, like the Latin *inhonestus*.

7. *Chæronea*. Philip of Macedon, father of Alexander, set out to subjugate the free states of Greece. The army of Athens and her allies was defeated by him at Chæronea in 338 B.C., and this battle marked the end of their independence. There is still to be seen a marble lion which was set up as a memorial on the site of the battle.

8. *with report,* by the news of it.

8. *that old man eloquent:* Isocrates, a famous Athenian orator. He is said to have starved himself to death four days after the battle (the same interval as with the Earl). He was, however, ninety-eight years old at the time, and the story is in any case doubtful.

There is also a parallel between the Earl and Isocrates, in that Isocrates had hoped that Philip would bring back unity and good government to the Greek states, and was disappointed in his hopes of Philip as was the Earl in his hopes of Charles.

9. *later born than to have known,* born too late to know.

10. *by,* through.

v. To the Lord General Fairfax at the Siege of Colchester

Sir Thomas Fairfax was an outstanding soldier on the Parliamentary side. He took part in the battle of Marston Moor (1644), and was in command at Naseby (1645), the two battles which decided the defeat of the Royalists, though it was not till the next year that Fairfax succeeded in crushing them completely. After two years of peace, however, there were fresh Royalist risings in Wales and in Kent, while the Scots sent an army to help the King, in violation of the 'Solemn League and Covenant.' Fairfax defeated the Kentish forces at Maidstone, and the remnants of them joined with others from Essex, and occupied the walled city of Colchester, which Fairfax proceeded to besiege; it was surrendered on August 27, 1648. Meanwhile Cromwell, after defeating the insurgents in Wales, met and defeated the Scottish army at Preston on August 17 of the same year. This sonnet was evidently written after Cromwell's success at Preston and before Fairfax's capture of Colchester.

Fairfax had a high reputation on account of his remarkable personal courage. (Although Commander-in-Chief, he rode through the fiercest of the fighting at Naseby, bare-headed.) But he was neither a great strategist nor a politician; and, in spite of his successes, he gradually retired into the background as Cromwell's influence grew.

In this sonnet, as in the last, we may well marvel at Milton's ability to write poetry in the very midst of such events taking place so near to him.

4. *that daunt remotest kings.* Causing them to fear similar successful revolts among their own subjects.

5. *virtue,* valour, the meaning of the Latin word *virtus.*

7. *Hydra heads.* See note on *Comus* (605).

7. *the false North:* Scotland.

8. *her broken league:* the 'Solemn League and Covenant' entered into by the Parliament and the Scots in 1643.

8. *imp.* A techinical term in falconry, meaning to graft new feathers on to broken ones in a falcon's wing.

8. *serpent wings.* The Hydra is not winged in the Greek legends, but winged serpents or dragons are frequent in romances, and the Hydra might be classed with them.

9–14. After the success of the Parliamentary cause corruption of every sort was general, and there was much petty tyranny among government officials. Milton in his prose complains bitterly of this state of affairs. Fairfax was quite unable to fulfil Milton's hope that he would put a stop to it (l. 9).

VI. TO THE LORD GENERAL CROMWELL
on the Proposals of Certain Ministers
at the Committee for Propagation of the Gospel

The Committee for Propagation of the Gospel was set up by Parliament early in 1652. One of its first duties was to decide under what conditions unofficial religious teaching and preaching might be given, and with this in view to examine the proposals of a plan put forward by fifteen ministers. Under this plan unofficial teachers were only to be allowed to speak in certain specified public places, and after obtaining the permission of a magistrate; and they must accept certain fundamental principles of the Christian religion. It was also provided that they must first obtain the sanction of two orthodox ministers, so that in practice anyone not acceptable to the clergy would be prevented from speaking at all, and no ideas not strictly conforming to the accepted creed could be put forward. It was evidently this last provision which most roused Milton's anger. He addressed the sonnet directly to Cromwell himself, who had indeed already spoken strongly in favour of freedom and toleration in matters of religion.

1. *a cloud.* Virgil speaks of "a cloud of war," *Æneid* (X, 809).

5–6. In these lines Milton seems to typify the house of Stuart, fallen from its former glory, over whose prostrate form Cromwell erects a trophy in token of the victory of the true religion.

6. *trophies.* See note on *Il Penseroso* (118).

7–9. Cromwell's chief victories were:

> *Darwen.* I.e., Preston (1648). See note on the Sonnet to Fairfax. The Darwen is a stream flowing near Preston.
>
> *Dunbar,* where he defeated the Scots in 1650.
>
> *Worcester,* where he defeated the Scots who had come to the help of Charles II, in 1651.

9. *laureate wreath:* the laurel crown of the victor. Cromwell called the battle of Worcester his "crowning mercy."

12. *secular chains.* Because the proposals of the ministers would have brought in the civil power to uphold their religious ideas.

14. A line full of scriptural allusions and echoes—"hireling" reminds us of the hireling shepherd of St John (x, 13), though it also refers to the eagerness of some of the Presbyterian clergy to secure paid posts for themselves; "wolves" recalls the wolves in sheep's clothing, St Matthew (vii, 15), and other instances of the metaphor. Milton himself several times refers to dishonest ministers as wolves, e.g., *Paradise Lost* (XII, 508).

14. *maw:* belly. Cf. *Lycidas* (114). A variant of the expression "whose God is their belly," Philippians (iii, 19).

The last two lines rhyme, this being the only such instance in the sonnets.

VII. ON HIS BLINDNESS

This is the first mention by Milton of his blindness. He had already lost the sight of one eye in 1650, but in spite of this, and against the warning of his oculist, he insisted on carrying out the request of the Council of State to answer the attack made on the Republicans by Salmasius. This he did in his *Defence of the English People*, after writing which he became completely blind.

It has been thought that this sonnet was not written till 1655, because in the first edition it comes after that on the massacre in Piemont. But this is not a necessary conclusion, and it seems much more likely that the present sonnet was written in 1652, when blindness first overtook him. It reflects the first feelings of despair when his affliction fell upon him, changing to patient and obedient resignation to the will of God. Later he found that he was after all not helpless or useless, but, on the contrary, his greatest work was done after he became blind; and he claimed that his mental sight and power was actually greater because of the loss of physical sight. The change is seen if you compare this sonnet with that on the same subject addressed to Cyriac Skinner in 1655.

The phrase "ere half my days" is in any case an exaggeration, as even in 1652 he was already forty-three; but if it had been written in 1655 the exaggeration would have been glaring.

2. *dark*, to a blind man. Cf. *Paradise Lost* (VII, 27), speaking of himself, "In darkness, and with dangers compassed round."

2. *wide*, terrifying in its boundlessness to a blind man. Notice how this is emphasized by the alliteration.

3. *that one talent.* Referring to the parable in St Matthew (xxv, 14–30). In a letter to a friend enclosing the sonnet *On His being arrived to the Age of Twenty-three* Milton had referred to the same parable and "the terrible seizing of him that hid the talent."

4. *useless.* Notice the tremendous emphasis thrown on this one word by the pause in the line.

7. *day-labour*, probably suggested by St John (ix, 4): "I must work the works of him that sent me, while it is day: the night cometh, when no man can work." In Milton's case, the night of blindness.

8. *fondly*, foolishly. Cf. *Il Penseroso* (6).

12. *thousands*. I.e., of angels. Cf. *Paradise Lost* (III, 650–653), where angels

> Stand ready at command, and are his eyes
> That run through all the Heavens, or down to th'earth
> Bear his swift errands over moist and dry,
> O'er sea and land.

13. *post*, travel swiftly.

14. *They also:* perhaps other angels, or perhaps men.

14. *wait*, in the sense so frequent in the Bible, of "waiting on the Lord. This is one more of the few familiar quotations found in Milton.

VIII. On the Late Massacre in Piemont

The victims of the massacre were the Waldensians (also called Waldenses, Valdenses, or Vaudois), a sect founded by Pierre Valdes in the twelfth century. They professed a simple Christian faith, of which poverty and charity were the chief points. Nevertheless, they were excommunicated in 1215, and so came to be regarded as the earliest Protestants. (Later an effort was made to show that they originated so far back as in Apostolic times.) Owing to persecution they gradually gathered in the remote valleys of the southern slopes of the Alps, over which the dukes of Savoy ruled. In 1561 they had been allowed to live in certain of the higher valleys, but ordered to leave the lower places. Gradually, however, they drifted back to these, and in 1655 the Duke of Savoy ordered them to leave, and sent an army to enforce the order. After clearing the lower villages the soldiers were billeted in the upper valleys, where on April 24, 1655, they carried out a sudden and cruel massacre. Many of those who escaped this perished in the snows of the high mountains, but some made their way to safety in France, and others gathered in remote spots and eventually formed themselves into an army. When Cromwell heard of the tragedy he sent a strongly worded protest to the Duke of Savoy, and also letters to the kings of Denmark and Sweden, to the Dutch Republic, the King of France, and others. These letters were written (in Latin) by Milton himself, as he was at that time secretary to the Committee of Foreign Affairs, and they can still be read in his Letters of State. Partly no doubt owing to the strong feeling aroused abroad, but also to the military successes of the Waldensians themselves, the Duke made peace in August, granting them their former rights. But the promise was never fully carried out, and his son made war on them again in 1689, again without success.

3-4. An allusion to the antiquity of the Waldensian sect, which was then believed to date from Apostolic times. In *The likeliest Means to remove Hirelings* Milton speaks of "those ancientest reformed churches of the Waldenses—if they rather continued not pure since the apostles."

4. *stocks and stones.* Referring to the statues in the pre-Reformation churches, which the Puritans considered no better than idols.

7-8. Sir Samuel Morland, who was the bearer of the letter to the Duke of Savoy, records this cruel deed in a book he wrote on the history of the Waldensians.

10. *Cf.* "The blood of the martyrs is the seed of the Church" (Tertullian, one of the early Fathers of the Church).

12. *the triple Tyrant:* the Pope, whose tiara has three crowns.

14. *the Babylonian woe.* The Protestants identified the Roman Church with the Babylon of Revelation (xvii and xviii). Here Milton also has in mind a sonnet of Petrarch (to which he refers elsewhere) attacking the Papal court. "Woe" may mean the destruction which is to overtake the Babylon of Revelation, but it is more likely that Milton is thinking of Petrarch's phrase "fountain of woe" in the above-mentioned sonnet.

Throughout this sonnet the strength of Milton's horror and anger makes itself felt. The very sound of the verse, with its repetition of *a* and *o* sounds, produces this effect.

IX. TO MR LAWRENCE

The "Lawrence" addressed in this sonnet was Edward, elder son of Henry Lawrence, a statesman and author of theological works, who was Lord President of the Council for some years. The son frequently visited Milton, and evidently had studious tastes. He became a Member of Parliament, but died in the following year at the age of twenty-four.

This sonnet shows Milton in a gay and cheerful mood. There are a good many echoes of Horace in it.

1. *virtuous*, of outstanding ability, intellectual though also moral. A Latin meaning.
4. *waste*, spend.
4. *what*. I.e., 'gaining what may be won' (making the best of the bad weather).
6. *Favonius:* the west wind, bringing in the spring.
6. *re-inspire*, breathe upon again.
8. *The lily and rose.* Cf. St Matthew (vi, 28), "Consider the lilies of the field, how they grow; they toil not, neither do they spin."

The point of the words "that neither sowed nor spun," in this particular place, is that the lily and the rose may serve as examples from nature to man in the opposite sense to the familiar example of the ant and the bee—*i.e.*, that there is virtue in pleasure and relaxation in their season, as well as in hard work.
10. *Attic*, simple and refined ("light and choice"), such as the Athenians approved.
12. *Tuscan*, Italian. Florence, the capital of Tuscany, was at this time famous for its musical and artistic life.
13. *spare To*, refrain from, a Latin idiom.
14. *oft*. Emphatic: he is not to indulge in these pleasures too often. So "sometimes" in l. 3.

x. To Cyriac Skinner

Cyriac Skinner was the grandson of Sir Edward Coke, Chief Justice of the King's Bench and the most eminent lawyer of his time, who wrote several books on legal subjects. His father having died young, his mother brought him up, and sent him to study under Milton, who at that time had pupils living with him. Skinner was Milton's favourite pupil, and remained one of his most intimate friends, living near by, and looking after him when he was in considerable danger at the time of the Restoration. He shared Milton's political views, and was much interested in politics, and also had literary friends, though he did not write himself. He was a lawyer by profession.

This sonnet is in the same tone as the last, and also has echoes of Horace.

2. *Themis:* goddess of Justice.

4. *bar:* law-courts.

4. *wrench,* distort.

6. *after,* afterwards.

7. *Euclid . . . Archimedes:* Greek mathematicians.

8. *the Swede:* Charles X of Sweden, at that time carrying on wars first against Poland and then against Denmark.

8. *the French* were fighting the Spanish in the Netherlands.

9. *To measure life. I.e.,* see it in proper proportion.

These lines mean that Skinner is to lay aside for the moment his study of mathematics and foreign politics. They are directly modelled on the opening lines of one of Horace's *Odes* (II, 11), in which he urges a friend to cease worrying about the intentions of the "warlike Cantabrian and Scythian."

XI. To Cyriac Skinner, on his Blindness

1. *this three years' day,* for three years. *Cf.* "I saw not better sport these seven years' day," Shakespeare, *2 Henry VI* (II, i, 2). This statement makes the date of the sonnet 1655.

1-2. Milton says the same thing in the *Second Defence* (1654): "At the present time, my mind is the same as ever, my strength the same, but my eyes not so. Yet they are in outward appearance unimpaired, as cloudless, clear and bright as those of men who enjoy perfect sight."

8. *bear up.* Verity points out that this does not merely mean 'endure,' but is a nautical metaphor meaning 'to sail,' 'take one's course towards,' and compares Shakespeare, *The Tempest* (III, ii, 3), "Bear up, and board 'em."

10. *conscience,* consciousness.

11. *In Liberty's defence:* in writing his *Defence of the English People.*

13. *masque.* Milton's variant of "All the world's a stage."

XII. ON HIS DECEASED WIFE

In 1656 Milton married as his second wife Katherine Wood-
cock. The marriage was a happy one, but the young wife died in
1658, after giving birth to a child which also died soon after.
Milton was already blind at the time of his marriage, so had
never actually seen his wife.

1. *saint*, both as a saintly character in her life, and as a soul
   in heaven; *cf.* "new welcome saint" *Epitaph on the Marchioness
   of Winchester* (71).

2. *Alcestis*, wife of Admetus, King of Pheræ, had offered to die
   instead of him. Her offer was accepted, but Heracles chanced
   to arrive just after her death. After a struggle with Death he
   brought back Alcestis and presented her to Admetus, who at
   first did not recognize her as her face was veiled. The story
   is the theme of Euripides' play *Alcestis*.

3. *Jove's great son:* Heracles. In Euripides' play Admetus
   addresses him as "noble son of almighty Zeus" (Jove).

5–6. The Hebrew law ordained ceremonies of purification
   after the birth of a child.

9. *vested all in white*. An allusion to Revelation (vii, 13–14).

10. *Her face was veiled*, as was Alcestis's in the play. Or Milton may mean that he could not see her face distinctly in his
   dream, as he had never actually seen her in life.

10. *fancied sight*. Milton was able to see in dreams, as blind
   people often do.

14. *my night*. His blindness returned when he woke.

APPENDIX

THE CONCEPTION OF THE UNIVERSE IN THE SEVENTEENTH CENTURY

THE theory of the structure of the universe current in Milton's time was that called the Ptolemaic system, after the astronomer Ptolemy of Alexandria (second century A.D.). It went back in some respects to Plato or even earlier, but had been added to and altered during the Middle Ages. According to this theory, the earth was the centre of the universe, and was motionless; it was, however, known to be round. Surrounding the earth were the elements of water, air, and fire, in that order.

The most remarkable part of this theory was the idea of the spheres, which was introduced in order to account for the apparent motion of the stars. There were eight spheres, which were transparent, but sometimes regarded as material, surrounding the earth at different distances, one within the other. To these spheres were fixed the stars. The spheres constantly revolved, carrying the stars with them. The seven innermost carried the seven 'planets' then known—the moon, Mercury, Venus, the sun, Mars, Jupiter, and Saturn; the eighth carried all the fixed stars. The general circular movement was caused by the outermost sphere communicating its movement to those within, and so causing the succession of day and night, of months, and of years. The irregularities of the planets were explained by supposing that each sphere had a separate movement of its own, apart from the general circular movement. Later a ninth sphere, the 'crystalline sphere,' was added, to account for the changes of the equinox, and later still a tenth, called the 'First Moved.' Milton usually recognizes nine spheres, though he mentions the tenth in *Paradise Lost*. The innermost of the planets was the moon, whose sphere marked a division between the heavier and grosser regions below (the earth and the elements) and the lighter and finer one above (the realm of the æther).

Copernicus published in 1543 the theory called after him, in which he demonstrated that the sun and not the earth was the centre round which the planets, including the earth itself, revolved. Galileo's discoveries (1610–16) confirmed this, so that by Milton's time it was well known. But the old ideas still persisted. So for example in a pamphlet written by some of Milton's associates, the authors, wishing to make clear the absurdity of their opponents' arguments, say, "There is no more truth in this assertion than if he had said with Anaxagoras 'Snow is black,' or with Copernicus 'The earth moves and the heavens stand still.'"

Milton himself had met Galileo in Italy, and it seems clear that he greatly admired him, and was considerably impressed by his discoveries. In *Paradise Lost* (VIII, 66–178) the archangel Raphael explains the constitution of the universe to Adam, giving the impression that the Copernican theory may well be right, but telling Adam not to think too much about these difficult problems.

But, though Milton may have been inclined to believe the new ideas to be the right ones, he naturally followed the old and established ideas in his poetry. He could, indeed, hardly have done otherwise, just as a poet of to-day would not introduce Einstein's discoveries into his poetry, even though he might know them to be true. It is not the business of poetry to popularize new discoveries, however important, but to make use of ideas which have a long history, and which have meaning and associations for his readers.

The Music of the Spheres

From this theory of the universe there sprang the idea or myth of the 'music of the spheres,' which came to be a favourite theme in poetry. The theory goes back to Pythagoras, a Greek philosopher and religious leader who lived in the sixth century B.C., and was taken up by Plato, who gave it a poetical colouring; originally it was purely mathematical.

It was supposed that the various heavenly bodies must make sounds by their movements. The sounds varied according to the distance and velocity of the stars which made them, and were determined by the laws of musical intervals, so that the whole series of notes produced a complete octave. ('Harmony,' in the phrase 'harmony of the spheres,' is used in the ancient sense of a musical scale, not of combined notes, as now.)

This music is the 'soul of the world,' and holds the universe and everything in it together. It is repeated in the soul of man, if that is in tune with the soul of the world.

Later the music was supposed to be produced by the revolutions of the spheres rather than by the movements of the individual stars; Plato introduced the idea of the sirens seated on the spheres and singing.

Although the music might in theory be heard by men, it was usually thought to be inaudible, either because, being continuous, it was not noticed, just as the noise of the forge is not noticed by a blacksmith; or else because the human soul is of inferior and earthly substance and therefore not in tune with the soul of the world. This imperfection later came to be regarded as a religious and moral, rather than physical, imperfection.

It is interesting to read what Milton himself said about the theory in one of the speeches he had to deliver as part of his academic training at Cambridge. This was *On the Harmony of the Spheres*, and in it he says:

> After all, we may ask, why should not the heavenly bodies give forth musical tones in their annual revolutions? . . .
> What if no one on earth has ever heard this symphony of the stars? It does not therefore follow that everything beyond the sphere of the moon is mute and utterly benumbed in silence. The fault is in our own deaf ears, which are either unable or unworthy to hear these sweet strains. . . .
> The fact that we are unable to hear this music seems certainly to be due to the presumption of that thief Prometheus, which brought so many evils upon men, and robbed us of that happiness which we may never again enjoy so long as we remain buried in sin and degraded by brutish desires; for how can we become sensitive to this heavenly sound while our souls are bowed to the ground and lacking in every heavenly element? But if our souls were pure,

chaste, and white as snow, as was Pythagoras' of old, then indeed our ears would ring and be filled with that exquisite music of the stars in their orbits; then would all things turn back to the Age of Gold, and we ourselves, free from every grief, would pass our lives in a blessed peace which even the gods might envy.

The Cosmic Dance.

Closely connected with the idea of the music of the spheres is that of the universal dance. The movements of the heavenly bodies were often thought of as a dance set in motion by the heavenly music, and this dance in turn was reflected in the tides of the sea, the dances of men and other creatures on earth, the movements of trees and flowers in the wind, and so on.